Praise for "7 Marketing Basics"

Cindy's book, "7 Marketing Basics," might be the most concise and precise presentation of marketing basics ever written. These seven elements of marketing are so concisely and succinctly presented that, whether you take one or take them as a whole, they will help your marketing efforts.

— Chris Krugler
Silicon Valley Marketing Consultant

"7 Marketing Basics" is very engaging and highly readable. If you are looking for a marketing book written in everyday language with plenty of guidance for business owners, this is it! The Bonus Materials and Resources are worth the price of the book. Highly recommend!

— Barbara Jones
Small Business Automation

With her "7 Marketing Basics" book, Cindy takes something that's big and scary for many people and makes it easy and — dare I say it? — FUN! This book encompasses something I can only call "the Cindy magic," and I love it! The book very coherently puts in place everything Cindy has done since we started working together, and it really helps me understand what's behind every campaign, suggestion, and question she ever asked me.

— Danna Mann
Director of Marketing Operations & Events
TAG V.S.

What's refreshing about "7 Marketing Basics" compared with other marketing books in this genre is that Cindy charmingly relates her methodology with many real-world examples of the situations and day-to-day challenges facing business owners. You can't help but have a wide grin on your face and be convinced after reading her techniques. A highly recommended read, this book is a valuable guide to marketing for entrepreneurs and small-business owners who want to be successful in today's competitive market. It is concisely written with easy-to-follow steps and bonus templates taken from Cindy's proven success formula.

— Saifudin Sani
Entrepreneur and Tech Expert

The tools and tips that Cindy shares throughout "7 Marketing Basics" are actually life-changing. Not only does she share them, but she teaches you in a way that anyone can understand. Her perspective on these marketing basics is enlightening and most of all, encouraging.

— Lindsey Ardmore
Business Strategist and Automation Expert
Star Tower Systems

Cindy understands that the key to success is providing simple, meaningful information about products, technology, and the market to your prospects and customers. She knows what works and what doesn't, and her guidance can bring real results in terms of visibility and sales. Cindy has the right approach to modern marketing in today's over-communicated-with-no-real-substance world, and "7 Marketing Basics" presents some of her best techniques and tactics.

— Stephane Billat
General Manager
DekTec America

"7 Marketing Basics" narrows down simple, actionable steps that are sure to set you up for success with a solid foundation for marketing your business.

— Jillian Littlejohn
Sparkle Solutions

Cindy is living proof of her "do less and double your results" strategy. She's the minimalist of marketers, keeping what matters and getting rid of the rest. No wonder she always looks so relaxed. She's on to something.

— Carol White
Owner/Web Designer
Winter Street Design Group

Cindy's "7 Marketing Basics" really hits the mark for marketing teams of any size or focus. By breaking down processes that can sometimes seem daunting or too time-consuming into simple, manageable tasks, this guide makes repeatable marketing ROI achievable for so many. And that's the key that so many of us marketers forget, unfortunately, when we're so caught up in ticking off to-do items. It's all about converting our marketing efforts into new customers and sales. Cindy has presented a plan that will help you ensure you're staying on the right path.

— David Cohen
Vice President, Marketing Communications
Grass Valley

"7 Marketing Basics" delivers on the content's promise, and its writing style is wonderfully friendly, engaging, and easy-to-read. I definitely learned from this book, and it has me thinking how I could better market myself.

— Bob Kovacs
Filmmaker, Videographer, Editor and Tutorial Maven

"7 Marketing Basics" is great. It is easy to read and authentic, reading just the way Cindy speaks. It's so cool that she has written a book on her passion, and she has done it well. The white paper section is excellent, and the webinar section is very, very good. In fact, I liked learning about all seven of the Marketing Basics.

— Kevin M. Joyce
Zer0 Friction Officer
TAG V.S.

Every year, many new marketing books are released, and most of them present a complex and confusing "Rah! Rah!" message that would require an army and a lot of money to execute. It is refreshing to read a marketing book that is not only excellent and sensible but also easy to read. Anyone who runs a small business (like I do) can learn and execute the thoughts and ideas presented in "7 Marketing Basics."

— MC Patel
Serial Entrepreneur
CEO of Emotion Systems

Cindy Zuelsdorf has taken the complex world of digital marketing and broken it down in easily actionable steps. With her "7 Marketing Basics," she's shown you exactly what to do when you're part of a smaller staff that wants to make a big impact in less time. By reading this book, applying the learning, doing the Marketing Basics Challenge, and tracking your results, you'll see that you're spending fewer hours focused on marketing tasks while making a greater impact. This will be one of the best investments you make all year! Thank you, Cindy, for sharing your wisdom with us yet again!

— Shell Vera
Voice Discovery Coach and Writer

7 Marketing Basics

Do Less and Sell More

Cindy Zuelsdorf

DEDICATION

To all of you entrepreneurs, small-businesses owners, and digital
marketers out there shining, excelling, and kicking a**!

TABLE OF CONTENTS

MY MARKETING EYE-OPENER

*What did you learn today? What mistake did you make
that taught you something? What did you try hard at today?*

— Carol S. Dweck

My entry into the world of marketing was … memorable. My first day on the job, I was ready for anything. But still I was surprised when my new boss walked in, handed me a grocery bag full of business cards from recent trade show, and said, "Think you could make a database out of these?"

As it happened, I had experimented a lot with building databases, and it all worked out fine. But what strikes me most today is how far we've come in handling leads and customer data.

Few of my experiences tell this story better than one of my first trade shows in Las Vegas. I still remember how we all met up in jeans and T-shirts to pack all the booth materials and equipment into crates to ship to the show. And then how we got out our Makita drills at the convention center to get lids off the crates and get our booth setup. We had a startup mentality, which meant we did everything ourselves.

We put on our nice clothes, did our meetings and demos throughout the show, and then changed back into jeans and T-shirts and scrambled to take it all down again. We got the crates ready to go, and I grabbed the leads everyone had gathered, as well as the data from the show's lead gathering company, and started my 9-hour drive home from Vegas.

Back in the day — and still today — it was important to get leads to the sales reps as quickly as possible. Being a young go-getter and overachiever in sales and marketing, I focused on getting the leads to the reps who were most proactive and productive and whose products were doing well at the moment. (Later I realized that I had been applying the 80/20 rule without knowing it. More on that in a minute!)

So, halfway home, I pulled into some cheesy motel in middle-of-nowhere Nevada to start typing leads into my computer. Fueled by coffee from the MiniMart next door, I was up until 3 in the morning entering data. It was a bit too much like a scene from a scary movie, so I did take a break to call my sister, get some moral support, and make sure someone knew my location — and that I was still alive.

I couldn't tell you the name of that motel, but I'll never forget the hours I spent sitting on that little bed surrounded by notes on various prospects. The name of the contact and company, their budget, the project they're working on, their timeline, their challenges, and so on. I put all that into the database, sorted it by territory, and made a mini spreadsheet for every sales rep.

I knew which sales reps were hottest and who I could count on to start follow-up immediately the next morning. These were usually the 20% of sales reps who brought in 80% of our sales, so I made sure they got the leads they needed to keep the momentum going. But I had to stay up half the night to get it done because I didn't have a solid plan and I didn't have solid systems.

Can you relate to any of this? Have you ever experienced this kind of overwhelming feeling?

Wow, have things changed since then! (And thank goodness for that.) We have better tools for capturing and organizing valuable data about our prospects, and the data is so much more complete.

Marketing automation has made it easier to prep for a show or online event, easier to collect useful information during the event, and easier to feed new contacts into your marketing machine.

These days, thanks to my Lifecycle Marketing Master Plan and to marketing automation, I can do much of my prep work as I travel to the event. I can then collect details, add notes, and tag contacts on the fly during the event. Best part: I'm done with my first round of follow-up before the event or show is even over.

If you are in charge of the marketing where you work and want to stop spinning your wheels so that you can step into a bigger role for yourself ...

or if you own your own business but you want to stop guessing what works ...

This book is for you!

If you want to discover and focus on marketing that really works so you can literally do less and double your results, read on!

PART ONE:

The Why

PART ONE:

INTRODUCTION

80/20 MOVES THE NEEDLE

80/20 says 80 percent of your results come from 20 percent of your efforts, and 20 percent of your results come from the other 80 percent.

— Perry Marshall

In working with hundreds of clients on their marketing, time and time again I've seen people trying to do 100% or 150% of everything. They are pulling out their hair, feeling overwhelmed by the sheer magnitude of trying to do it all, and frustrated by not knowing how to be more efficient and effective with their marketing efforts.

But things have changed…

You've heard about the Pareto Principle: **80% of your results come from 20% of your efforts**.

But have you put this same 80/20 rule to work in your marketing? (If you want to learn a lot more about it, check out Perry Marshall's book, "80/20 Sales and Marketing.")

Have you really tried it? Here's the thing: 20% of your marketing efforts deliver 80% of your sales.

What we'll talk about throughout this book is how you can focus on that 20% of marketing efforts that yield the results you crave. Yes, you can stop guessing and lean into what works.

I still remember the time, not too long ago, that I was talking with a business owner (now a friend and client) about the 80/20 rule. You should have seen the relief on his face when we got to the part about not needing to do 100% or even 80% of all possible marketing tactics! His shoulders relaxed, and he was able to take a deep breath and reset his thinking.

Like most business owners, he's already got a lot on his plate. He'd rather work on developing new products and services than on marketing, but he knows marketing is critical to the success of his business. What he understands now — and has embraced wholeheartedly — is that by focusing on the right 20% for his business, he can move the needle in a big way.

And this part of our conversation is worth repeating here:

You don't have to do it all. You just need to find the 20% of marketing efforts that will move you toward your business goals.

Embrace that idea, and you'll move the needle for your own business. You will be able to focus on the 20% that will produce 80% of your results.

Here's what this friend said to me later:

"A year ago, I could not work out how we could reach the masses. We had a great product, but we were struggling. And then, you and I talked!"

He recalled our conversation about the 80/20 rule and recounted how it changed his thinking and his approach to marketing. He told me that within the 12 months since we had spoken, the 80/20 model had transformed his marketing. His business has seen real sales results.

We've all seen people at small and medium-sized companies working terribly hard, regularly putting in 12+ hour days. Maybe that's us?! These dedicated business owners and marketers miss out on working smarter because they are simply too busy to stop and "sharpen their tools," too busy to make their company better.

Many of these same companies seem reluctant to use technology in their marketing systems because they are afraid it will make them feel impersonal. They've always sold in a certain way and are worried that a system would change the organic way they do business. They figure it just won't work.

But I've seen firsthand that really good sales and marketing systems can determine the success of a company… and be the difference between good and great. I've watched modern marketing tools — and marketing automation in particular — help companies augment the work of the sales team, bolster their success, and provide enhanced services to customers. Such systems create repeatability and success.

Now, I'm not saying it's easy to stay current with the latest marketing trends and tools. Maybe you don't have the time, or maybe it's just hard to make it a priority. Even when you're a marketing professional, it can be difficult to put the latest tools together in a way that helps you and your business take marketing through to sales.

If you're like most marketers out there, you could use a hand — some insider knowledge and a few shortcuts to save you time and make your marketing efforts pay off. That's where this book should come in handy.

The book is divided into two parts. In Part One, you'll learn about "the why." You'll find out about the Lifecycle Marketing Master Plan and how it can help you assess your current marketing activities. Applying this plan to your business, you can see opportunities to better align your efforts with your goals.

If you feel you already have a good framework and a solid understanding of your situation — or you're just eager to get started! — feel free to skip ahead to Part Two, which focuses on "the how."

In the chapters that make up Part Two, you'll learn about the 7 Marketing Basics — and how and where you can put them to work for your business. These are the marketing tactics that make up that 20% that can bring in your 80%.

Looking at some of the fundamental principles that should guide your marketing efforts, this section of the book reviews seven of the most important tactics used in marketing today. Next, you'll take a deep dive into three simple but important ways you can drive more effective marketing for your business.

Finally, we'll discuss tools and systems that help you leverage your efforts to their fullest potential.

As you dig into the following chapters, remember that it is possible to do less and achieve more with your marketing! By the time you get to the end of this book, you'll know where to focus your time and energy — how to do less AND move the needle.

CHAPTER 1

SIZING UP YOUR SITUATION

If you are going to reach your destination, you have to take your first step. Of course, it does help if you have great shoes.

— Kim Walsh-Phillips

As you prepare to focus on that 20% of marketing that can really move the needle for your business, it's helpful to step back and look at your sales and marketing strategy as a whole.

Do you have a coherent and cohesive strategy, or are you just working with bits and pieces here and there?

Maybe you have invested some time and money in your website at some point, or you've taken a stab at reaching out through Facebook and LinkedIn. Perhaps you have sent out the odd newsletter or shared a favorite graphic via email.

All these things can be part of an effective sales and marketing strategy, but only if you have orchestrated use of these tools and tactics so that they are focused and targeted to the audience most likely to become your customer.

So, before we get into using those tools and tactics, let's take a quick look at how you can assess your current situation. Do you take a clearly defined and consistent approach to getting more leads, working with your prospects, and increasing sales in an efficient, time-saving way? (Yes, the 80/20 principle again!)

If you feel you have a handle on these things and just want to get started, go ahead and skip ahead to Part 2 of this book! You can always come back to learn more about the Lifecycle Marketing Master Plan, which is the tool that I rely on and many of my clients use as a guide and yardstick for measuring up our business.

Lifecycle Marketing Master Plan

I first heard about lifecycle marketing from Scott Martineau at Keap / Infusionsoft, and it totally resonated with me. I adapted it, made it my own, and have used it as a primary framework ever since.

When you use the Lifecycle Marketing Master Plan to evaluate your business, it reveals where the opportunities (or holes) are so you know what to do next and how to prioritize. It's my map, my guide, the ultimate business framework — and now it can be yours, too!

The Lifecycle Marketing Master Plan is built on three main pillars, or phases: attract, educate and sell, and wow.

When you have solid marketing strategies and tactics deployed in each phase of the Lifecycle Marketing Master Plan, then your business will excel! Following this plan allows you to establish a

28

unified and continuous process for guiding prospects toward a purchase and driving ongoing engagement.

Holes = Opportunities

In this next section, as we look at each part of the Lifecycle Marketing Master Plan, take note of where you have holes, or opportunities, in your company. I suggest that you literally take notes as you read. Write in the margins of this book! Or make a note on your phone.

You'll be using these thoughts and insights as you move into the next chapter of this book, and your future success!

And, in case you're wondering, you're not alone here. We all have holes and opportunities in our businesses.

Target + Attract

Before you can target your prospects with your marketing, you need to know them. That's why identifying your ideal customer persona is the first phase of the Lifecycle Marketing Master Plan.

Who are your customers? When you think about the last 10 or 20 people who bought from you (or the first 10 people you'd like to buy from you). How old are they, where do they live, what problems do they have, what are their values, and what do they want?

Capture whatever information you can and then categorize prospects by their interests, behavior, demographics, location, and any other detail that differentiates them as potential customers. By putting these categories together for a particular type of prospect or customer, you are creating a persona or ideal customer avatar. If you have two or three perfect customers, come up with a distinct name for each one.

Next, identify how they find you. What information would be incredibly helpful to them, and what would draw them in? Using your ideal customer personas as a guide, you can move forward in providing prospects with the right messaging and information on the right communications platform.

You can use your own experience with current customers to define your ideal customers. At the same time, tools such as your website and marketing automation can help you identify prospects who, in doing their research, have shown interest in your business, products, or services.

Collect Leads

When someone is interested in working with you, how do you capture their data? It's crucial to have a simple and good way to collect your leads. Can you snap a photo of their business card on your phone and bring them right into your database? Can you have someone fill out a form on your website or Facebook and send them directly into your database? We all need to have a really good system in place that lets people join our group, our tribe, our email list, whatever it is. Make it easy for people to indicate interest, sign up, or join!

Educate + Help

Once someone raises their hand and indicates interest, how do you educate and help them? You want to create an experience where your perfect customer can learn something from you. You could provide emails, videos, other great info that addresses typical objections. When people talk with you or message you with questions, what are the things people always ask? If you can help them, be of service to them, then they will be more likely to buy from you. Be the expert! They will get the info they need from someone – why not from you?

Offer + Close

How are you set up for offering and selling? If you're all set here, that's great. But there are so many people who need to work on this piece.

If it makes sense for your business, do you have a good way for someone to try out what you offer, maybe download something that you offer, or some way for them to check out what you are selling?

Is it easy for them to buy, is pricing clear? Can they easily send you a payment or is it difficult? Further, it's good to have a system in place for the times that your prospect doesn't follow through to make that first payment.

Wow + More

I like to call this Wow + More because first, we need to deliver the purchased product or service as promised, and second, we can look at ways to over-deliver. So your customer says, "Wow!" You can add that special touch they will appreciate and remember, plus distinguish yourself from other companies and competitors.

Can you give them a quick call and find out if they liked their appointment? Can you send them something really wonderful that they wouldn't expect — chocolates, a book, something custom they'd love? What can you do to help them to like you even more? And how can that system be automated so it happens every time?

Ultimately, by wowing your current customers, keeping them happy and coming back for more, you not only build loyalty but also set yourself up for testimonials and referrals, which is a fantastic way of getting new business.

Get Referrals

We all talk with friends and colleagues before we buy. So, doesn't it make sense to have a plan in place to automatically get reviews, Google stars, and referrals? Yes!

Everyone can benefit from having a system in place to ask for reviews on Google, Facebook, Yelp, or wherever your customers hang out. NPS, or net promoter score, requests can go out to customers asking for ratings and input. And if we need to improve, it's good to know that, too. It's wonderful to have a system in place that ensures everyone is happy and we're spreading the happiness.

Scan with your smartphone for a special video.

The Lifecycle Marketing Master Plan in Action: A Service Business and a Software Business

When you think about your sales cycle, do you look at it in terms of "Attract, Educate + Sell, and Wow?"

It's a proven framework, and you can discover a bit more about it here and see how to apply it to your business. Below, in the first of two examples, you see how the owner of a service business might use the Lifecycle Marketing Master Plan.

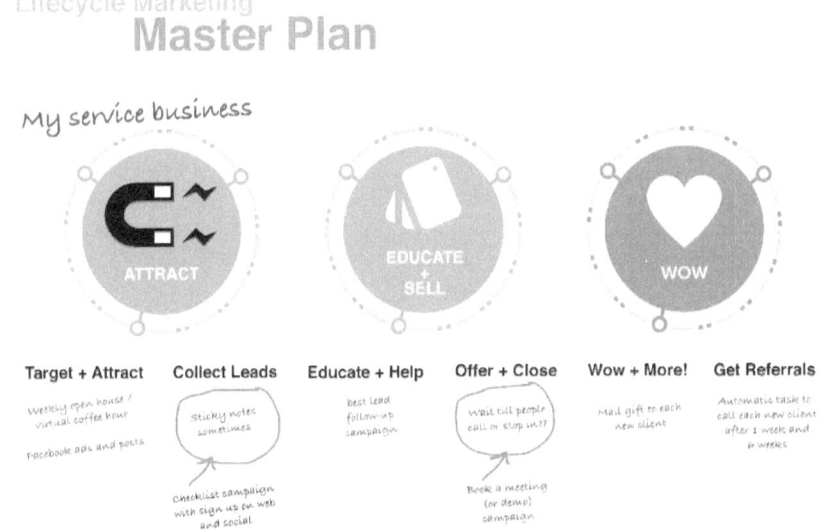

Example 1: Service Business

If you have a service business, you should definitely use the Lifecycle Marketing Master Plan to evaluate your company. Here's an example based on a real-life client we've worked with.

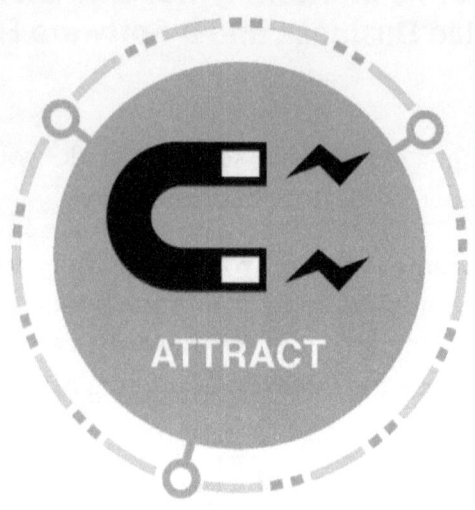

Target + Attract

Weekly open house / virtual coffee hour

Facebook ads and posts

Collect Leads

Sticky notes sometimes

Checklist campaign with sign up on web and social

You already know that prospects are on your website doing research and deciding if you're on their short list or not. But do you know who they are? And how will you connect with them?

People do up to 70% of their research before contacting you. Can you afford not to know who they are? Use marketing automation and find out who your prospects are while they are in the research phase — your Attract phase!

Educate + Help

best lead
follow-up
campaign

Offer + Close

wait till people
call or stop in??

Book a meeting
(or demo)
campaign

Does this sound familiar?

"My salespeople focus on the deals that are closing in the next 60 days. I've got leads falling between the cracks. What can I do with the 'warm leads,' the people who need education and info but don't have budget yet? How can I keep them thinking about my products and services?"

People need to connect with you up to seven times before they are inclined to buy. And they want info that is specific to their projects, not a general list of all the great things you offer.

Wow + More!   Get Referrals

Mail gift to each
new client

Automatic task to
call each new client
after 1 week and
6 weeks

Do you ever wonder this?

"Is there a simple way to sell more, get a lot of referrals, and be sure my current customers are happy?"

Yes! One of the top indicators of future success is how customers feel about your business. When your customer wants to refer you to his or her friends and associates, it's a signal that your business will do well in the future. You can automate Net Promotor Score (NPS) surveys to your customers and be on top of this key performance indicator.

Example 2: Software Business

If you're in charge of marketing for a software business that sells products, you should absolutely adapt the Lifecycle Marketing Master Plan as a framework for your business model.

Here's an example based on a software company we worked with. Does any of this look familiar to you?

Page ahead to see each element in more detail! (You can also find a large-scale version of this graphic — with helpful notes — in the Resources section at the end of this book or get it here: https://7marketingbasicsstart.com.)

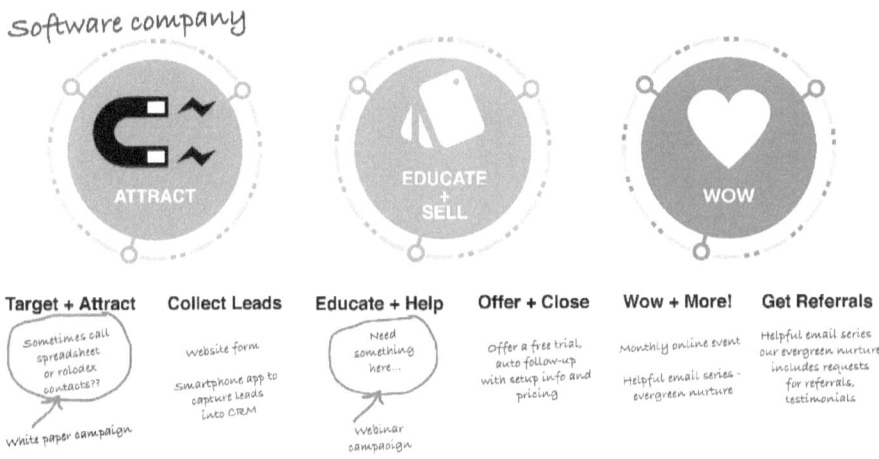

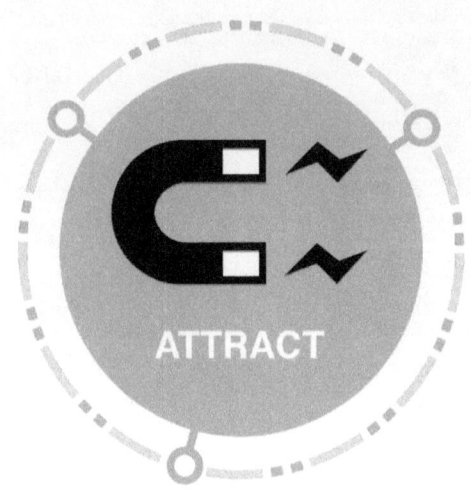

Target + Attract

Sometimes call
spreadsheet
or Rolodex
contacts??

White paper campaign

Collect Leads

Website form

Smartphone app to
capture leads
into CRM

Do you sometimes think this?

"I know prospects are on my website doing research and deciding if we're on their short list or not, but I don't know who they are. When I buy something, I do pretty much all my research online before I buy. My customers must be doing that too. Is there a way for me to know who those people are?"

Use the Attract phase to reach out and offer the info your prospects want and need.

Educate + Help

Not doing much here, but I should!

webinar campaoign

Offer + Close

Offer a free trial, auto follow-up with setup info and pricing

What will you do with contacts on social media or the leads you gather at the next trade show or online event?

Use marketing automation to send your prospects a series of emails and videos that are super-targeted and useful to them. Use Educate+Sell to make sure prospects are predisposed toward you when they are ready to buy.

Wow + More!   ## Get Referrals

Monthly online event

Helpful email series -
evergreen nurture

Helpful email series -
our evergreen nurture
includes requests
for referrals,
testimonials

Repeat business, upselling, referrals, and testimonials can all be automated to your advantage.

Know, Like, Trust

While the Lifecycle Marketing Master Plan offers a crucial framework for generating leads and seeing customers through and beyond the sale, the Know, Like, Trust relationship plays a vital role in cementing your connection to current and prospective customers.

I'm not sure exactly when I first heard the Zig Ziglar quote about "Know, Like, and Trust," but I love talking with my clients about this idea. In fact, this approach is so successful so often that I finally formalized it into a campaign that most of my clients now use.

The Know, Like, Trust approach I have refined over the years is built on the idea that relationships are at the center of sale. It draws on the buyer's journey and ties right into your Lifecycle Marketing Master Plan. But at its core, Know, Like, Trust is about making and sustaining a connection with your prospects and customers.

Naturally, you begin with the "Know" element – help your prospects get to know you. You might introduce yourself in a brief video or two where you talk about a recent project and the problem you helped to solve. In doing so, you begin to give prospect a sense of who you are, and you also show them that you the expertise to understand and address their challenges.

Over time, by connecting through these short video clips and by providing information related to your prospects' industry and the specific challenges they face, you will get into the Like and Trust part of your relationship. You offer value and expertise, and it becomes clear to prospects that you are invested in your customers' success.

I'm all about the abundance mindset. It's important to deliver first, before asking something of the prospect in return. Not everyone agrees with this, but I feel that if your prospects like what they're getting — and feel they are already getting a helping hand from you — then they can move forward and make a purchase at some point down the road.

Marketing automation (Keap/Infusionsoft, ActiveCampaign, HubSpot, and others) can support this process. As prospects engage with the content you supply — video clip, website, email, blog post, etc. — the automation system can capture those leads and apply lead scoring that informs next steps. Prospects can be automatically funneled into further engagement, such as a demo or consult, based on their previous interactions.

If the score gets to a certain threshold, your automation system can alert you or a salesperson through a simple email or notification that it's probably time to get in touch and start a conversation with a particular prospect.

The Know, Like, Trust approach offers a natural progression for generating leads and guiding them into an ongoing relationship with you. At the end of this process, you can automatically shift prospects into an "evergreen" campaign that keeps your business in their awareness and nurtures the relationship you've already built. You continue to offer tidbits of value or interest, always giving prospects the option of engaging once again for further information.

Being Your Authentic Self

In my experience, the Lifecycle Marketing Master Plan and Know, Like, Trust only work when you combine them with authenticity. Makes sense, right?

And while you may be genuine in your intention to help people solve specific problems, you may not find it easy to connect in an authentic way.

One way I work with clients to overcome this challenge is to do a quick video chat about a recent sale or installation and about the problem they helped to solve. The conversation usually starts something like this: "The other week I was at a client site and …."

If you start by talking about a typical pain point or problem, you can show that you understand the issues facing your customers. After focusing on the problem for 80% of the time, you shift to the solution. Then you can provide more detail or additional insights in a one-to-one appointment or product demo.

Creating and sharing a short video in this format will help you show your authentic self — the person who has invested time and energy in addressing and solving customer problems — with all those little quirks or habits unique to you. And it invariably does get prospects following up for more information. It's awesome!

Summary

Now that you've looked at your business and what you have in place for each phase of the Lifecycle Marketing Master Plan, the holes, or opportunities, should be clear. You likely see one or several areas of your business that need your attention. And that's good. Read on for the next steps!

Chapter 1: Quick Review

- 80/20 Rule, Pareto Principle: 80% of your results come from 20% of your efforts.

- Lifecycle Marketing Master Plan — the ultimate framework for your business. Shows you holes and opportunities.

- Know, Like, Trust. As Zig Ziglar said, "If people like you, they will listen to you, but if they trust you, they'll do business with you."

- Perfect customer, ideal customer avatar, persona. Define and name them.

- Holes = Opportunities. Find what's missing or needs work in your business when you compare it to the Lifecycle Marketing Master Plan. Start there.

- Target + Attract

- Collect leads

- Educate + Help

- Offer + Close

- Wow + More

- Get referrals

- Be your authentic self

➡☐ Get started by downloading the Life Cycle Marketing Master Plan here: https://7marketingbasicsstart.com As you go through this book, fill out the Master Plan and let it be your guide   to   success!

➡☐ Join the 7 Marketing Basics Facebook group here: https://www.facebook.com/groups/7marketingbasics/.

PART TWO:

The How

CHAPTER 2

GETTING DOWN TO BASICS

Don't just identify the problem; find a solution.

— Liz Wiseman

Now that we've set out the Lifecycle Marketing Master Plan framework and you've taken note of where your biggest holes (opportunities!) are, let's get into the 7 Marketing Basics themselves. I've learned a lot from thinking about and applying the Lifecycle Marketing Master Plan, and Know, Like, Trust, and you can too.

But you don't have to!

Thanks to the 80/20 rule, we know that it's not necessary to know every aspect of each framework intimately. You just need to identify and focus on the 20% of marketing that can yield 80% of your sales.

I realize this isn't easy in today's digital marketing landscape. If you were to outline all possible avenues for reaching out to prospects and clients, the result might look like the popular Web Strategy diagram created by David Meerman Scott. (You can find a larger version in the Resources section at the end of the book.)

The diagram highlights dozens of different ways that a business might connect with prospects. It points to the numerous tools that businesses can use to guide people along the journey from prospect to satisfied customer.

Don't get me wrong. I love this diagram, and so do many of my clients. But incorporating all these elements into a cohesive marketing plan can be a bit much to think about all at once.

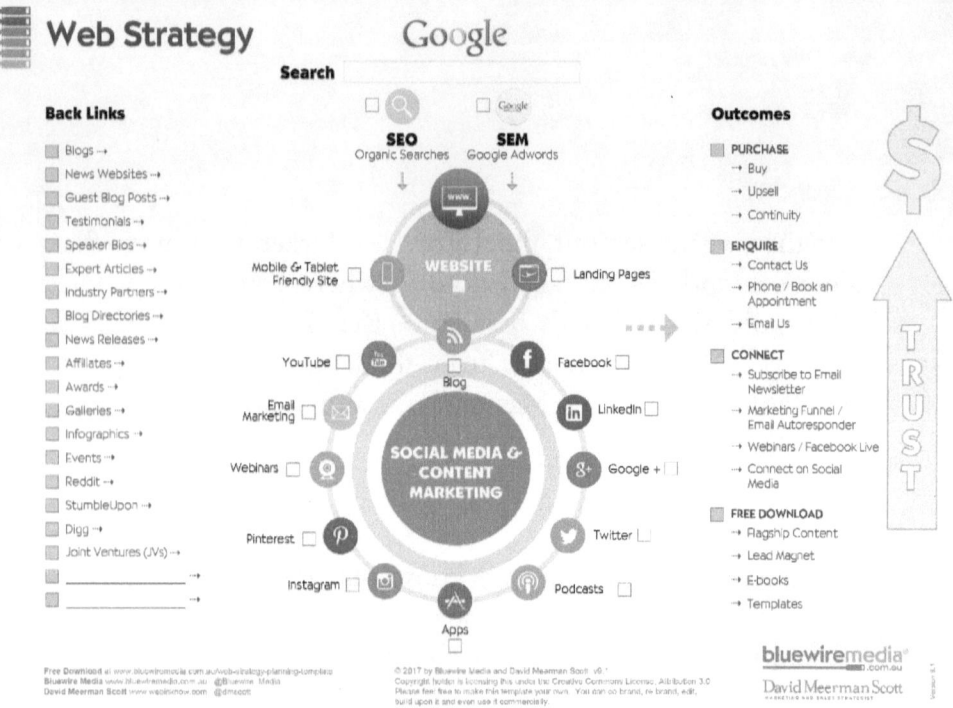

If you read this diagram from left to right, you see the broad array of things you can do as part of a digital marketing strategy. At left you see the "get to know you" elements of the strategy, and as you move up and to the right, you work your way to the sale.

I have seen clients try to tackle all the elements on this diagram. They needed to get results, but they got overwhelmed when looking at this massive menu of things they could be doing. They found they were spending too much time on their marketing or simply not getting results that made the work worthwhile. In the end, many just felt lost.

My message to clients in this situation is simple: Don't do it all.

Sure, you do need a website or, at a minimum, a Facebook business page, just like you have an accounting system or even just a phone number. You need a place on the web to send people.

But you don't need to live a life of experimentation and try every single thing all at once. You can narrow your focus to a short list of marketing basics that just work. Put your energy into tried-and-true tactics and tools.

Do less! Just do the 20% that brings in 80% of the results.

Now that you know where the opportunities are in your business, it's time to decide which tactics to apply. You can use one of the seven basics to patch the hole, or leverage the opportunity, in your company. So, let's get into the seven!

Proven Winners: The 7 Marketing Basics

In working with hundreds of people and companies with my digital marketing agency over the past five years, I certainly had an idea of the elements that were working best for them. But the picture really came together for me once I took the time to sit down and identify the tactics that virtually guaranteed success for my clients.

My family had cleared out after our traditional Thanksgiving gathering, and I had some unexpected free time to look over past projects with my clients. Armed with sticky notes in various colors, I sat down at the dining room table and mapped out the tools I had used with each client.

Narrowing the possibilities from dozens to just a handful was easier than I anticipated. I asked myself, "What are the tools that really work for my clients?" And then, "When people call for advice on how to use various marketing tools, which do they ask about most often?"

Ultimately, I hit upon 7 Marketing Basics, with each one being a tool or tactic that can be implemented on its own or along with others for a more extensive campaign. Now, I'm not saying there isn't an eighth, but these seven have proved to be the most popular and consistent because they work!

The 7 Marketing Basics

No. 1: Sales From a White Paper or Guide

No. 2: Webinar

No. 3: Social Media (basics)

No. 4: Lead Follow-up (best practices)

No. 5: Virtual Trade Show or Event Promo

No. 6: Evergreen Nurture Campaign

No. 7: Meeting, Demo, or Trial Request

Each of these 7 Marketing Basics meets two key criteria. First, it falls within the 20% of marketing tactics that will get you the greatest results. And second, it is simple and straightforward enough that it can be implemented with relative ease.

In other words, each Marketing Basic allows you to increase the impact of your marketing efforts while reducing the work you put into them. And what's really exciting is that you can combine these basics to increase impact and maintain momentum. It's important to have multiple touches all along the sales funnel, and these 7 Marketing Basics give you a system for making those critical connections. (Learn more about the sales funnel in the Bonus Materials and Resources section at the end of the book.)

If you have found yourself wondering why the marketing you've been doing for the past 5, 10, or 15 years is not working anymore, it may be the right time for you to jump into these 7 Marketing Basics.

No. 1: White Paper/Guide

The white paper/guide is a great starting point because it leads to immediate engagement. A quick win! Right away, you get people talking with you. And you can get going quickly because you can more or less start with what you've already got plenty of: expertise.

Look through your files, and you'll probably find something that, once you make a few quick changes or drop it into nice template, can be a valuable asset. Chances are that you've already documented your expertise in an existing guide, manual, or video that addresses customer concerns or challenges.

Whenever you offer valuable information, it can be a great way to help people know, like, and trust you. So important.

No. 2: Webinar

Like the white paper campaign, a webinar can help you to present your expertise in a way that will attract potential customers, offer them value, and invite them into a conversation. This might be a great starting point for your businesses as you take your marketing up a notch.

The webinar might showcase expertise in the form of a person, such as a colleague with an unusual depth of knowledge and/or a knack for explaining how your company's solutions solve customer problems.

If you implement these first two Marketing Basics in your Lifecycle Marketing Master Plan, then you can use other Marketing Basics to keep the prospect moving toward the sale. Focus on the 20% that'll get you 80%.

No. 3: Social Media

I've added social media to my top three Marketing Basics for many reasons. It can be a valuable tool for getting new leads and for connecting at various points along the customer journey. And honestly, it's something most clients feel they need to do, but often don't know how to do!

Whether or not you choose to dive into social media — Facebook, LinkedIn, Twitter, Instagram, and so on — you will benefit from understanding how these platforms can support your marketing efforts. As you make connections on LinkedIn, Facebook, and other platforms, you give prospects the opportunity to opt in and become part of your community.

No. 4: Lead Follow-up

Lead follow-up is one of my favorite Marketing Basics because it focuses on taking prospects further into the sales funnel rather than letting them fade away.

Too many times I've seen marketing folks gather leads from an email blast or a trade show and then simply dump them in the lap of whoever is in charge of sales. The marketing folks move on to the next marketing task while the salespeople follow up with the hottest leads — the people most likely to buy in the next month or two. Oftentimes, both sales and marketing forget about all the "cooler" leads and allow them to fall through the cracks.

When I see this, it almost breaks my heart. So much money is being left on the table! Those leads are worth pursuing. Don't let the work that was done to make those connections go to waste. And don't get so focused on generating new leads that you forget about the perfectly good leads you've already captured.

No. 5: Virtual Trade Show/Event Promo

A lot of businesses use events and trade shows (in person and virtual) to stay in touch with existing customers and to get new customers. In fact, I've seen some clients spend the bulk of their marketing budgets on these events. And now there's an even bigger shift toward digital or online events.

But it only makes sense to put in all this work and money if you plan marketing tasks that will help drive traffic and make the event a success. It's a no-brainer, which is why it's among my 7 Marketing Basics.

No. 6: Meeting – Demo – Trial Request

What does your prospect do right before they buy? Do they usually set up a meeting with you, ask for a demo, or in the case of some online products – download a free trial? Or, to put it another way, when your prospects engage in a meeting, demo, or trial, what percentage of the time do they buy? Is it a high number? You need a system in place for the thing your perfect customer does right before they buy.

A company we work with told me that 79% of the people who did a software trial of their product ended up purchasing. Guess what we did next – put a system in place to offer the free trial to everyone who came to a webinar, downloaded a guide, or visited the website. Sales went up!

No. 7: Evergreen Nurture Campaign

The evergreen nurture campaign is a great way to maintain those regular touches that are important to keeping prospects aware of your brand and solutions. In a way, this campaign is a little bit like a newsletter, in that emails go out regularly to people on your target list.

What's different is that this type of campaign focuses more specifically on talking about problems your prospects might need solved. It is "evergreen" because the information in each email is useful, but not so timely that it becomes dated or irrelevant.

Like many others, this Marketing Basic is about being a resource. You're offering potentially useful information and then just saying "Hey, if you need any help, reach out any time." At the same time, you're educating prospects about your business, and maybe even letting them know about products and services they didn't realize you offer.

Keep up an evergreen nurture campaign, and you're never going to lose touch with people who want to hear from you — people who might be ready to be a customer in the future. As you move forward with other marketing efforts and continue to generate new leads, you simply drop new contacts into this campaign and allow them to cycle through the series of email messages.

Just last week a client told me they got an email reply via their evergreen campaign. The prospect needed some services, and my client ended up with a sweet deal. This works!

The 7 Marketing Basics and the Rule of 70

Your prospects do as much as 70% of their research online before they contact you. Probably more. Can you afford not to know who they are?

The Rule of 70 came from our experience of seeing that customers do at least 70% of their research online before they buy. I sure do! You, too, right? We look around online, go to a website, maybe check with friends in Facebook, Instagram, looks at YouTube, etc., before reaching out to a company or raising a hand to show we're interested. We need to jump in and make the most of the Rule of 70 and put it to work for ourselves!

By incorporating the 7 Marketing Basics into your marketing, you can engage with your prospects while they are researching, while they are deciding who's on their short list and who's not. You can send them relevant, helpful information, specific to what they are interested in. Keep educating them, keep them thinking about you, and when they are ready to buy, they'll want to buy from you.

Summary

These 7 Marketing Basics really work. They help you focus on the 20% that will get you 80% so that you can do less and still be more effective.

Marketing should bring new sales. (Otherwise why do marketing, right?) Focusing on specific tools and tactics, the 7 Marketing Basics will empower you to move forward with creative, engaging, and effective marketing initiatives and campaigns.

In the chapters that follow, you'll learn more about these powerful tools and exactly how to get started using them — and get results! We'll focus on three of tried-and-true favorites: the white paper/guide, the webinar, and social media basics.

☐

Chapter 2: Quick Review

- Apply the 80/20 rule to your marketing. Stop doing everything. Do less! Just do what is proven to work.

- David Meerman Scott's web strategy diagram shows the myriad marketing tactics in use today.

- 7 Marketing Basics — Seven strategies and tactics that work.

  1. Sales From a White Paper, Guide, or Checklist

  2. Webinars

  3. Social Media (basics)

  4. Lead Follow-up (best practices)

  5. Trade Show or Event Promo

  6. Evergreen Nurture Campaign

  7. Meeting, Demo, or Trial Request

- Rule of 70 — Your prospects do as much as 70% of their research online before they contact you.

➡☐ Join the 7 Marketing Basics Facebook group here: https://www.facebook.com/groups/7marketingbasics/.

CHAPTER 3

THE WHITE PAPER, GUIDE, OR CHECKLIST

Don't fear sharing your best ideas online.
1) Competition already knows what you are up to.
2) People like leaders not followers.

— David Meerman Scott

As you know — and we've discussed already — creating a connection with your potential customers is an essential part of the sales process. I'm a firm believer that if you are of service and provide value right out of the gate, you can change a person's perception of you, from the very beginning. You help them know, like, and trust you.

While it requires that you be kind of a patient marketer, the guide, check list, or white paper campaign is a great way to offer this value and start building that deep connection with folks. It can be any kind of asset really — a guide, checklist, video, or other knowledge asset.

A white paper, for those wanting a definition, is generally a document that gives in-depth detail on a technology, concept, or service, but is not salesy.

Anything that provides information or answers will be useful to your prospects. You might be surprised to find that you've created and filed away quite a few different kinds of documents and presentations you can leverage in your campaign.

This is a great way to generate new leads and to reengage your cold leads, so it fits into a few places in your Lifecycle Marketing Master Plan. (And, to put it in context cost-wise, you can do this kind of campaign for less than you'd spend on one print ad!) This type of campaign also allows you to educate your prospects and help them understand why your product or service should be part of their thinking as they look to the future.

Often, the response from your prospects is "Wow, this person just gave me value. And they didn't ask for anything!" The second time you get in touch, they see you're again offering value, and they start to see you as someone who is just trying to help them out. You become an ally!

Give people the information they crave. They're going to get it from someone, so **why not you**? Be the expert!

Creating a Four-Step Campaign

After you've selected the checklist, video, guide, or white paper that will serve as your knowledge asset, you're ready to plan your campaign. (For the sake of simplicity in discussing the campaign, let's just say the asset in question is a guide.) I like to call it the "pinnacle piece." No matter what kind of content you choose to use, you can incorporate it into this kind of campaign.

The campaign is built on four basic steps.

Step One: Get It Out There!

Promote your free and super useful guide to all the people you know. Send it out to your house email list to see if people like it. This is a great way to test your pinnacle piece. You might get a great response right off the bat. Or, you might hear some feedback that suggests a few modifications might be in order. If so, no big deal. You can iterate and make tweaks as needed.

Once you feel you've got the guide in shape, you're ready to progress to step two.

Step Two: Extend Your Offer

You've tested your guide with a warm, friendly crowd. The next step is to promote that asset to people you don't know. You could do a paid email blast through an industry or trade magazine, do Facebook posts and ads, or use LinkedIn. You could try paid advertising, create a pop-up on your website, or just include the offer in the signature of your email.

The link you offer will send people to a landing page for your guide. As people sign up to receive the guide, you can use an automated system to capture contact details directly into your CRM or database and automatically deliver the guide.

Step Three: Follow Up on Your Offer

Your campaign is really rolling now. To keep the momentum going, design a new email series for those folks who took you up on your guide-download offer.

Start with a thank you email. It can be short and sweet — a simple acknowledgement for your prospect. You're showing how thoughtful you are, and you're normalizing emails from you and your business. If they opted-in by text, then send a text.

Next, create several more email or SMS messages that build on the guide. In this series of follow-up emails, offer information that will help prospects to consume that information, apply it, and be successful with it. Remember that by opting into the guide, they expressed an interest in your product or service and they may want more.

One option is to take some of the content from the guide and restate it. People are busy and they might not read the full guide, or might not read it all at once. It's just fine to remind them of that helpful information in a friendly and conversational way.

Be sure to include an ask or call to action in these emails. If something low-pressure is your style, that's fine. Just make it clear to the reader what the next step should be, what you want them to do next. Maybe it's just to call with any questions, or to try a live demo. Whatever the case, any customers who take that next step in the sales funnel can automatically be excluded from further follow-up mailings. Marketing automation (email or SMS) will push them into a new phase of marketing while continuing the campaign for people who haven't yet responded.

By providing these automated tools and processes, automation does more than simplify your campaigns. It helps you to ensure that prospects don't fall through the cracks and that promising leads get the attention they deserve. When you're doing the work to generate leads, this is important! You don't want to create an opportunity for your business and then miss out because some part of the process fell apart.

Step Four: Close the Loop

When you build a call to action into your follow-up email or SMS series, be ready for those folks who decide to take action! At this point you might want to set up an automated task that sends an email to the salesperson or a rep who will go ahead and arrange a call or do a demo. Be sure you've put in place a system for moving those prospects forward toward a purchase.

So, what does this type of campaign look like in real life?

Remember the client I mentioned earlier, with the white paper and the software trial? For him I just went into my marketing automation system and built a really simple campaign starting with two simple emails. Each email offered the white paper to existing customers.

Next, I used social media to offer the white paper to a wider group — a targeted group of people who were new to the company. Almost immediately, nearly 50 people clicked through and opted in to download the white paper. So far, so good!

Because the white paper was a fairly long document with a lot of interesting information, I took tidbits from it to create a series of nine emails. (OK, that's a lot – feel free to start with 2 or 3.) While content in the paper was written in the third person (and honestly just a bit stuffy), I turned it into a conversation with the email recipient.

"If you're dealing with this particular challenge, you might be interested in this solution." In addition to information or ideas that might be valuable to the reader, each email includes a call to action. For this particular client, the obvious CTA was to try the free software download.

We adjusted the campaign it a little bit over time, mostly to make sure the emails were responsive for mobile phones and to keep the content up to date. The campaign continues to offer content that the company's prospects value, and it still drives potential customers toward that critical step — the software trial — that might just lead to a purchase.

Among other things, this example shows that that you don't need to run dozens of campaigns to use marketing automation successfully. You just need to identify those one or two things that are really going to move the needle for you and then just be consistent about using them.

Refine this path over time and keep it working like a well-oiled machine. That's what creates results: one path that really works. Don't get stuck on perfection. Iteration is the key. You need to start somewhere, and you can always make it better and better over time. It's like a conversation you have with someone on the phone — it's not going to be perfect, but it's a starting point. Just go with it.

Not Quite Ready? Pre-sell Your Guide

If you are just about to finish up your guide, white paper, or ebook, but it's not quite done yet, you can "pre-sell" it by asking for advanced sign-ups.

One client I worked with wanted to do something to drive trade show booth traffic at an upcoming exhibition, but they didn't have any product to announce quite yet. We decided to promote an upcoming technical paper and asked prospects to sign up to get an early look at the paper. This was very successful, as it created buzz and provided a great way to find out who was interested in this new topic.

Campaign Summary

Promote your checklist, guide, or white paper through an email, on social media or on a website.

Start by promoting your free guide to the people you know. Then promote it to people you don't know through an industry magazine e-blast. When someone signs up for the guide, use an automated system to capture their info directly into your CRM and deliver the guide.

Send a series of follow-up emails that include excerpts from the guide and additional info that's on-topic.

Be sure to offer the person something more. They wanted your guide, right? Offer them something else that's beneficial. Every email in this sequence should have an offer, a call to action.

One client we work with offers a software demo. Another offers a product data sheet.

Automatically stop the follow-up email series if the prospect downloads the software demo or data sheet.

Design a new email series for those who take you up on your offer. Send a thank you email first, and then several more emails giving pro tips on how to set up and get the most benefit from the software trial, for example.

Set a task to follow up with the prospect by phone. You can also send out an automated email or SMS asking if the prospect wants to click a link and purchase, book a meeting, or start a demo.

Summary

What hole or opportunity do you have in your business that would benefit from this proven marketing basic? You could use a white paper, guide, or check list (lead magnet) to attract prospects and capture them into your database, to educate your prospects, or to wow your existing clients by teaching them some new information.

☐

Chapter 3: Quick Review

- Create a connection with your potential customers, help them know, like, and trust you.

- White paper — A document that gives in-depth detail on a technology, concept, or service, but is not salesy.

- Checklist — A list of steps to take, things not to miss, or points to be considered on a particular topic.

- Guide — A short document that provides info on how to do something. It usually gets someone started quickly and provided actionable information.

- Lead magnet — Marketing speak for any asset that gives value to your customer and can be given in exchange for contact info (email or mobile).

- WIIFM stands for "What's in It for Me" and refers to the fact that customers only really care about what's in it for them, their point of view, their wants and needs.

- Give your prospects the information they crave. They'll get it from someone — why not from you? Be the expert!

- Call to action or CTA — What you want your prospect to do next after they read your email, watch your video, or visit your website, for example.

- Pre-sell — If you are just about to finish up your guide, white paper, or ebook, but it's not quite done yet, you can "pre-sell" it by asking for advanced sign-ups.

➡☐ Join the 7 Marketing Basics Facebook group here: https://www.facebook.com/groups/7marketingbasics/.

CHAPTER 4

THE WEBINAR

If you don't think you're ready to teach someone, think again. The simple act of teaching will raise your expertise exponentially, in a way you didn't even think was possible.

— Ryan Levesque

Live webinars are a proven way to connect with your audience, build your list, and sell your products and services consistently. Webinars, webcasts, online meetings, and virtual events turn your marketing into sales.

But most folks feel like doing a webinar is going to be hard — that they'll have to spend a month preparing and need to put together 200 PowerPoint slides.

For ease, I'm going to refer to webinars in this chapter, but you can take the info here and apply it to your webcasts, online meetings, and virtual events, too.

Sure, you'll want a solid plan for driving attendance and making sure your webinar runs smoothly from start to finish. But you don't need to move mountains to make it happen.

I've helped many first-time webinar hosts plan for a webinar. I put together a plan that guided them through the process painlessly, and it might come in handy for you, too. It starts with some simple goal setting.

Whether you'll be introducing a new product during your webinar or discussing an important industry trend, it's all so much easier when you start with the end goal in mind.

In addition to defining this goal, consider these questions: What's the ideal outcome? Are you looking for sales? Appointments? Demos? Awareness?

Once you've answered these questions, it's time to get down to the details.

Start With Being Yourself

Before we dig into tactics, let me just share a quick story with you.

I was working with a client to orchestrate a webinar. He planned to have a few of his company's experts participate, and he knew from working with me how important it is to connect with customers and prospects in a genuine, authentic way.

This client said to me, "Remember when we first met to talk about webinars, and you just told me to be myself — to sound like a regular person, not like a press release or sales pitch? Can you do that for my team? Can you help them understand that?"

What I did with this client (and many others!) was to get the presenter on video and ask him to summarize what he'd be talking about during the webinar. We recorded it as a 30-second promo, and right toward the end, this particular guy sort of looked down for a split second and then back up at the camera again as he was talking. Somehow, that unique little mannerism suddenly made him so much more human and relatable.

You can't put it down on paper, but you know it when you see it! It's character, personality. Small moments like this resonate with customers because they are authentic.

This is just one reason why webinars are such a great tool. Customers will see you on screen and know that they're going to find out a bit about who you are. As you talk about how your product or solution solves a problem, you also reveal a little about yourself. You become someone they can talk to. They begin to know, like, and trust you.

For many people, this starts out as a daunting prospect. Maybe they don't like the sound of their voice or aren't used to being on camera. But I just say, "Tell me about the last time you picked up the phone and talked with a customer." For most folks, it was just the other day, and it's a conversation that is familiar to them. It happens all the time. And they wouldn't dream of not doing it! Talking to customers is part of what they do.

Sometimes I'll also ask about the time they did a demo for a customer, or chatted with a prospect who stopped by their trade show booth. Inevitably, there is some similarity across all these conversations, both in the way clients engage with customers and prospects and in the type of information they share. This kind of authentic interaction — a real conversation about real challenges and solutions — is exactly what makes for a great webinar.

What's my point in telling this story? You know this stuff already! Like the back of your hand. So, don't reinvent the wheel. Don't rehearse. Do not write a script. Keep a few talking points on hand if it makes you more comfortable, but remember that presenting on a webinar should be no different than any other personal engagement with customers.

One way to make a webinar more of a conversation than a presentation is to bring a colleague or fellow expert into the mix so that you can have a real discussion.

My clients have been doing joint webinars with partner companies, as well, and they're finding the cross-marketing opportunities — expanding their reach to a new and much larger audience — really exciting!

When doing the webinar with a friend or colleague is not an option, you can try a few other tricks to make it a more comfortable setting.

Some of my clients like to look off camera because they find it too weird or awkward to stare right into it. I generally suggest putting someone or something about 15 degrees to the side of the camera as a focal point, the way they often do in documentaries and for interviews for major network news.

Maybe you paint a face on a volleyball or have a friend sit in. The idea is that you feel more like you're talking to someone you know, and that your conversation sounds like a real conversation you might have when sitting down to talk with a real person.

The reason I recommend two people is that it's usually easier and more natural, and the format makes it less likely that you'll go into soapbox mode with your presentation. Not so fun for your webinar guests. That said, if you have a knack for going it alone, great!

You totally can do a webinar solo; just find the approach that feels most relaxed and works best in allowing you to connect with participants.

The first few times I did webinars all on my own, I experienced that isolated, talking-into-a-hole kind of feeling. But when I did a webinar with a colleague, I could see that person's eyes light up when I made a good point, and that told me I was on the right track. I got valuable feedback, and attendees understood that the conversation wasn't just a one-way stream of information and ideas.

You don't need to be an amazing speaker or entertainer to do a great webinar. You already know the subject matter and can speak to the needs of your customers. You just need to be yourself.

Pre-Webinar Planning: The Show Outline

Figuring out what your attendees care about and digging into the problems they have are great ways to determine the topic of your webinar. Decide what success looks like for you.

With your end goal in mind, identify the topic of your webinar. Maybe make a list of the value or benefits you expect it to offer participants. These notes will come in handy as you promote the event, and they also will help you stay focused in your planning.

This is also a good time to define your call to action. What do you want attendees to do after the webinar? Common CTAs are to sign up for a demo or appointment, make a purchase, download a checklist or a summary of the webinar's main points, or visit a website for bonus information. In the ideal circumstance, what would your attendee do next, following the webinar?

If you're doing a webinar with a guest, get on the phone or a Zoom call and chat briefly about what you both expect the webinar to cover. To make the process super easy for them if they don't already have a clear idea of what to say, you can ask what they'd do and say if they were sitting down for a face-to-face chat with a prospect or customer. Help them imagine a familiar and comfortable scenario.

During this preliminary chat, you can also explain how you plan to welcome attendees and make sure they start engaging and using the webinar chat box.

If your guest is open to questions from attendees, agree on how you'll take care of that. If you know your guest has a good story or two to tell, mention that you might ask about them if the mood seems right.

If you get the sense that your guest is a bit nervous about presenting, which people often are, you can assure them that you'll make them look good and help get through any awkward spots.

I created a guide called Webinar Tech Essentials that shows how to choose your tools and setup for your next webinar or online event.

Claim it for free by texting TECH to +1 530-203-5703.

Using notes from your conversation, go ahead and make a show outline. Begin with a show opening in which you welcome participants and introduce your guest, restate the topic of the webinar, and identify the top three or four things participants can expect to learn. Offer just enough detail to engage participants immediately and keep them interested.

In addition to creating a list of topics or points to be covered during the webinar, ask your guest about some questions you might add to the Q&A following the presentation. Just in case you don't get many questions — or all the right questions —

from attendees, work with your guest to create a few softball questions that will keep the conversation going through that Q&A period.

Write a show close for your webinar, remembering to thank everyone, including your guest, for attending. Provide contact information and any other links once again.

Determine what your call to action will be. What do you want attendees to do after the webinar? Sign up for an event? Download a summary of the webinar's main points? Download a demo? Visit a website for bonus information. This is your parting gift to each attendee, and you can use it to end the event on a high note.

Creating a Bulletproof Webinar Outline

- Get two people on to co-host so it feels easy and conversational. Both people are on camera and are connecting with attendees.

- Begin by chatting with the audience for the 10 minutes prior to the start of the webinar. Get them to engage and use the chat box.

- Start by welcoming everyone and telling them what they will learn/get if they stay with you for the whole webinar.

- Tell three stories, each illustrating a key point, application, or challenge. The stories help identify who you are for, what problem you solve, and what prospects should know about you. Feel free to mention your CTA.

- Open up Q&A time.

- Close and recap your three points and then restate your call to action.

See the Resources section at the back of the book for a complete webinar checklist.

Pre-Webinar Planning: The Technical Details

Like any production, a webinar requires some behind-the-scenes work. Before you get too far into planning, decide who is going to assist you during the webinar by managing the chat box, gathering attendee names and contact details, and giving attendees a way to interact with the hosts.

To ensure that everyone is on the same page throughout the webinar, give both your assistant and your co-host a copy of the show outline, as well as notes about when to display a particular URL, email address, or even an image or diagram to complement the discussion.

Even if you've successfully used Zoom or another videoconferencing technology in the past, make time for a rehearsal with your co-host, your assistant, and your technology. While Zoom and other tools do offer recording capability, and you should be sure to use those, I strongly recommend that you find a way to make a backup recording. I've only had to go back and re-record once, due to some technical glitch, and it was hard to talk my webinar guest into doing it a second time! Now we have a colleague do an audio/video capture using QuickTime, ScreenFlow, or a similar application.

During this planning phase, also talk with your co-host or guest and your assistant about how you'll communicate during the live event. You can use Skype, WhatsApp, text messages, or another back-channel communications tool to orchestrate the show. You'll want to mute new message alerts so that they don't disrupt the webinar. Also be sure that if one of you will be screen-sharing, you have closed any application that might deliver an unwelcome notification.

Check in with your co-host or guest and assistant to find out if they're comfortable with an abbreviated practice run, keeping the conversation fresh and spontaneous for the real webinar, or if they really need the full presentation mapped out. You'll probably want to run through the notes together at a minimum.

If you'll be using an interview style, you and your guest can choose to let the conversation go off-topic if it's an interesting and relevant tangent. Remember that the show outline will be there to help everyone get back on track.

However you decide to do it, practice enough that everyone feels comfortable and understands the plan. While a full run-through isn't necessary, a practice run can help you all iron out any wrinkles — and possibly prevent a relatively small issue from becoming a big problem during the live event.

Because not every webinar will run according to plan, be prepared for an unexpected disruption. Your guest may get called away for an urgent phone call, or temporarily lose audio or video. If this happens, you may need to step in and improvise a bit. This will be easier if you've thought about how you or your assistant might fill some down time until you can jump back into the session.

Of course, your practice run is the time to make sure that audio and video do work properly, that the recording function does in fact capture them reliably, and that the guest's backdrop, lighting, and camera angle are OK. Remind your guest to smile and pause from time to time, ideally at natural transitions between topics. You will be creating a webinar replay video from your live event, and little touches like this will make editing much easier.

How long should the webinar run? While some presentations can go nearly an hour, we've found that a 20-minute live webinar works great for most topics (and the attention span of most participants). You'll have another 10 minutes at the end that you can use for the Q&A or flex so that your guest can address areas of interest in a bit more detail. Let your guest know that you and your assistant will keep an eye on the clock and move things along if necessary.

Pre-Webinar Promotion

Once you have consulted with your guest, created show notes, and completed your rehearsal, you're ready to promote the webinar on social media. Use LinkedIn or Facebook to send people to an attractive signup page. You'll want the webinar title and a graphic, if possible, along with a headshot of your guest. You might want to add a bio for your guest, or even a snippet of video from your rehearsal call on Zoom.

I've found that I get great results if I can show the guest talking a bit about the webinar topic, what people will get from attending, and what they'll be able to do by the time it's over.

That extra bit of personality really engages folks and helps them follow through on registration.

Using text, email, or a combination of the two, confirm each attendee's registration and later provide a reminder or notification of the upcoming event.

If you take care of all these things prior to your webinar, you'll make it easy for your webinar guest to share their expertise and you'll help each attendee get as much out of the experience as possible.

During the Webinar: Getting the Show on the Road

Go ahead and start your webinar about 10 minutes early so that you can welcome attendees as they come online. This is a great time to put guests at ease with a few friendly questions about where they're from, and if the audio and video seem OK to them.

As your start time nears and more attendees join, point out the chat box and invite them to engage by providing a little information about themselves, the kind of business or industry they work in, or even what the weather's like where they are. Some videoconferencing services will provide chat content as part of a transcript, but it's wise to have your assistant record and annotate this information too.

While not everyone will contribute to the chat or conversation, you'll still create a shared discussion and get attendees comfortable with using the chat function. You'll also remind them, on a more subconscious level, that they are part of a live event.

Aim for an on-time start, with maybe a minute or two for everyone to get settled, and then launch into your show opening. Let attendees know how long the webinar will go, restate what they'll be learning, and remind them that a Q&A will follow.

After you've introduced your guest or co-host — but before you hand over the mic, so to speak — be sure to tell the attendees why they should stay and what they will learn. This first few minutes are crucial as your attendees are deciding if they like you and if they want to spend the next part of an hour with you or not. Tell them clearly what's in it for them if they stick around!

One more note: Always remember why your guests are there. You don't need to justify yourself or your webinar to people who already bought in! Offer them more of the value that persuaded them to sign up in the first place.

During the Webinar: Staying on Topic and on Time

As the webinar proceeds, follow along using your show notes. In addition to coordinating chat box questions and notes with your show assistant, you'll want to keep an eye on the clock. If your guest is spending too much time on a particular topic, feel free to step in and provide a transition to the next topic on your list. Alternatively, you can acknowledge how much there is to know about that topic and remind guests that they can post questions for the Q&A at the end of the webinar.

Whether your webinar is threatening to go over time or you're just barely stretching things out to 20 minutes, it's important that it has energy. If there is time, or a particularly good moment, a good anecdote can be a great addition to the webinar. People will remember a story. It shows some of your guest's personality, and it brings the conversation from the theoretical into the real world.

If your guest gave you permission to ask about a story or anecdote, and if you think it will enhance the discussion somehow, go ahead and set your guest up to add some color or humor to the conversation. "Which event were you at when …?"

Be sure to provide contact info for the guest on email, Twitter, Facebook, or LinkedIn in case attendees have further questions following the webinar. Or just put the info into the chat box, that works well, too.

During the Webinar: Nailing the Q&A and Close

Ideally, attendees will have posted questions to the chat box throughout the presentation, providing solid material for the Q&A. Don't forget about the backup questions you and your guest created during your planning session. While you want to answer attendees' questions, you'll also want to make sure that the Q&A touches on any topics that were promised but not fully addressed during the presentation.

If neither the guest nor attendees have anything new to add, pose some forward-looking questions that you discussed in advance with your guest. Conclude with some speculation on what might come next. Then, move into your show close.

After offering your thanks to everyone involved, provide your guest's website or contact details once again, both on-screen and verbally. You can also suggest links for further information or action. Use that call to action! End on a positive note by offering yet more value to webinar attendees.

After the Webinar

You did it! You finished the webinar, hopefully it was nice and smooth, without a major hitch.

If you had 50, 100, 500 people – great! But even if you had a smaller turnout, maybe just 10 or 20 people on the webinar, remember that if you set up a booth at a trade show, you'd be thrilled if just 10 people spent half an hour visiting and learning about your product or services. For a lot of companies, that's a pretty fabulous day. (Plus, you'll be leveraging the recorded webinar for months or years to come. You can spin it out into 50+ pieces of helpful sales and marketing content!)

Now, follow up on that success. Begin by sending a thank you to attendees. If you've already edited the video to create a webinar replay, you might offer them a link to it, or a cleaned-up transcript, or a summary of the presentation.

If the webinar promoted a particular product or service, attendees probably already know about your irresistible, high-value offer. Send a follow-up text message, asking attendees if they have a question you can answer. Help them take the next step in your sales funnel.

Even as you cultivate your relationship with webinar attendees, take the time to reach out to people who didn't make it to the event. With a simple "sorry we missed you" note, acknowledge that they're busy and let them know that some great things came out of the webinar. You can offer the webinar replay or a condensed version of it, just in case they have questions or know of anyone else who was interested but couldn't attend.

Summary

Webinars provide such a great way for you to connect with prospects and customers. Have you tried one yet? Go for it! Webinars and online meetings skyrocket Know, Like, Trust because the attendees can interact and really get to know you. Video is magic that way. You can use a webinar, or online meeting or event, to attract new leads, educate prospects, and grow your relationship with existing clients. It's one of the most popular campaigns we do with clients right now because the content can be used in so many ways – from the live webinar to evergreen replays and more. Jump in!□

Chapter 4: Quick Review

- Live webinars are a proven way to connect with your audience, build your list, and sell your products and services consistently.

- ID the goals of your webinar. What's the ideal outcome? Are you looking for sales, appointments, demos, awareness? What's the call to action?

- Figure out the show outline. Decide who the talent will be and what format you'll use.

- Decide on your tech: webinar platform, camera, mic.

- Do a rehearsal / tech check /run-through.

- Consider using a webinar chat master to take care of chat and engagement.

- Do the webinar! Be yourself, be conversational, deliver a ton of value.

- Webinar Q&A plan.

- Plan your promotion.

- Plan your follow-up.

- Use the webinar checklists in the Resources section at the back of the book.

➡️□ Text TECH to +1 530 203-5703 to get your Webinar Tech Essentials PDF freebie.

CHAPTER 5

SOCIAL MEDIA

Always enter the conversation already occurring in the customer's mind.

— Dan S. Kennedy

I was talking recently to a client with a small company — just 10 people in it — and we decided to do a quick video of him chatting about a new piece of technology and the problems it solves. We were already on a video call, so I was able to grab 90 seconds of our recorded conversation and turn it into a nice little video clip. All in all, it took maybe 15 minutes.

We put that video up on LinkedIn, and right out of the gate, he got 750 views and a handful of comments, including a request for a meeting. This is why social media matters!

Why Engage on Social Platforms?

Social media puts you where your customers and prospects are. It might be Facebook, or Twitter, or LinkedIn. Regardless, if they are there, you need to be there, too. Another important factor to keep in mind is that because the software and algorithms used by these platforms are smart, they can help get your message to people you didn't even consider might be interested in your product or service.

Sure, you talk on the phone with customers, exchange emails, catch up at trade shows, and so on. But if you're not meeting prospects on social media, you might be missing out on a huge opportunity. (And your existing customers could be wondering where you are.)

Wherever your customers are, you should be too.

1. Credibility

Once upon a time, people wondered if they really needed a web presence. Today there is no question. And the same is true for social media, which arguably has become even more important than a website to many businesses.

Social media is a uniquely effective tool in helping people get to know you, like you, and trust you. Here it is again: Know, Like, and Trust. It's a proven recipe for success. By providing insights and valuable information via your social media presence, you not only keep your brand and products visible, but also legitimize them. You establish credibility.

2. Authenticity

Much like credibility, authenticity supports a prospect's inclination to know, like, and trust you and your business. Social media always has excelled in allowing people to be authentic and share who they are. And your customers want to know who you are. Working with clients to refine their presence on social media, I've seen the most engagement when people are authentic about themselves and what they're up to.

If you're at a trade show or conference, offer a behind-the-scenes look at your booth setup. Tell a story about what it took for you to get there. If you're installing a new product at a customer's facility, show how you're working to make sure the job is done right.

You don't have to reveal some big secret in order to be authentic. You don't need to share client names. Just talk about the problems you see customers encountering and how your products are being used to solve them.

3. Social Proof

People buy from people they like. And they also rely on recommendations from friends and colleagues as they make purchase decisions. Comments, retweets, and likes on social media: all of it is social proof, and it can help your brand and business.

Where do you look online when you're going to buy something? If you're like most people, you have a few different places you'll go to check reviews, feedback, and ratings. You might start with a Google search or watch a YouTube video. These are the kinds of places you want your business to be!

What suits your personality and your products best? Consider Facebook, LinkedIn, YouTube for starters, maybe Twitter, Instagram, or Pinterest, and then expand to other social platforms out there. People are always looking to learn from the advice of others. Word of mouth now extends into social media, but you need to be there if it's going to benefit your business.

As you dig into social — or start to boost your current presence — find ways to ask people to join you.

Do you have your social links on your website, on your business card, in your email footer? Do you say to people, "Hey, connect with me on Facebook!" You'd invite people to an event or to register for a webinar. Now ask them to meet you on social media.

But What to Post?

Start out with simple posts. If you're struggling to come up with content for your posts, make a list of questions that you often get from prospective and existing customers. Nothing comes to mind?

Take a look at your email outbox and see what's there. Think back to your last event or demo. What questions did people ask? Any recent phone calls stick in your mind? In all that customer engagement, there are sure to be some great topics for your social posts.

While generating new ideas and new content for posts is great, chances are you have something in your files that you could grab from for a post or two. Have you put together a list of any kind, made a video, or written a guide or white paper? All these pieces of content must offer one or two ideas or solutions that would be of interest to your customers. Build some posts around them. Quote a snippet or two.

If you're short on ideas, you can also try the behind-the-scenes post. While it may not convey useful information, it will engage viewers' curiosity. Where are you, and what are you doing? What does your office or manufacturing space look like? And what's going on in the background? I've gotten likes for photos of me just sitting at my computer making a video. Instead of a closeup, it was a wide shot that showed the equipment I was using and how I created a makeshift studio of sorts. I was amazed at the response. People loved it.

Why does this matter? It's engagement, which is part of building a relationship. (Repeat along with me: Know, Like, Trust.) When people take the time to post a comment, thoughtful or funny, they are reaching back toward you, helping to build a connection that might one day lead to business if it's a fit.

Applications for your products or solutions are also a solid topic for your social posts. Tell a story — no names needed — about your last installation or project, and the problem you helped to solve. What was the challenge, what were the customer's requirements, and how did your product address them? For longer posts, use a conversational tone to tell the story.

Or, just make a quick video of yourself talking about the project and how it all worked out. If you haven't already, explore tools such as Facebook Live or LinkedIn Live. After a bit of experimentation, you'll get comfortable sharing a live conversation or trimming a recorded stream for posting.

If you're already a blogger, you know to look back over past posts. It's likely that you could use a single blog post as the basis for a series of posts. Lift enough content for four or five (or more!) posts and schedule them out over time. You don't have to come up with original material every time, just a different angle that might match up with the interests or needs of customers. Recent presentations and webinar can also offer up a wealth of valuable post material, as they often include diagrams and images that help capture attention on social media.

Social posts are a great way to offer promo codes for attendance at upcoming trade shows, parties and special events, or speaker series. You can highlight your own involvement and offer value to others who might be interested too. Even if you don't offer a promo code, you'll want to post in advance of any upcoming events. If you create a Facebook event, you'll automatically reach friends and followers with event news and updates. You can also use calendar links and booking links to encourage people to commit to (and remember) to attend events and meetings.

For every post you create, try to keep in mind what it is that you want someone to do after they read that post or watch that video. What are you hoping they do next?

With each post, you also want to give readers or viewers the opportunity to ask for more — and to get more from you if they want it. Go to the blog post and read more. Click this link to book a meeting with me. Follow this link for more detail on this particular specification. Put a call to action right in there, and make it easy to take action.

Should I Promote My Product?

To promote or not to promote? This is a great question.

How much should you promote your product when you post to social media? Some people say a good guideline is to offer four helpful, interesting posts for every post that includes a product pitch.

Because one goal of posting is to provide value to prospective customers, you might consider sticking with more helpful posts, less product pitch — and maybe even no product pitch. Just let people know that you understand their problem and what's happening with them. That alone can be enough for them to consider reaching out to you for a solution. As long as that call to action is in there in your post, you're probably doing enough promotion.

I like to think about it as if I were meeting a prospect in person. Would every other sentence be a pitch? How would that go over? Probably not so well. What would I really say face-to-face?

Your social media presence should be more of an exchange of ideas. You can provide useful information. You can ask how people are doing and if they need help with any particular challenges. Just be yourself, be authentic, be helpful.

How Do I Write It?

My friend Wes says that marketing is just sales written down. I love that. I've taken it to mean that when we're writing anything for our marketing, it should sound like a conversation, something we'd actually say to someone. So, in this case, if it doesn't feel natural when you say it out loud, it's probably not a fit for your social post.

With that in mind, write in the first person, using "I" when possible. This voice gives people the authenticity they want to hear from you. You may not be completely comfortable with writing this way, at least at first. That makes sense.

"I went to a company's headquarters yesterday and met with the CTO."

"When you talk to your next customer, you might ask them about…"

"So-and-so was just telling me about how to fix a recurring problem, maybe you've seen it, too…"

It's all about you! (And by that I actually mean "them.") Meaning, it's all about the reader and what's in it for them. However, so many of us have been trained to write in a very impersonal, third-person style and that feels so distant. When in doubt about taking this approach, just remember that it's the personal tone that gets more engagement. Posts that lean toward the personal and familiar get more shares, likes, and comments.

The idea is to connect! And by putting yourself out there authentically via your social media posts, you're offering people that connection.

I'm sure you're also wondering about hashtags, which have become a key element of posts on many platforms. They can be important in helping people to find your posts, and they are worth putting some thought into. If you want to get into the nitty-gritty details of choosing and using hashtags on various platforms, check out this link to some info about hashtags and best practices: https://sproutsocial.com/insights/hashtag-analytics.

What Kind of Images Work Best?

Go ahead and use photos you've taken with your phone. It's totally fine, and it's what people have grown accustomed to seeing. That said, if you're going to be prepping an image and getting it ready in advance, you can use the size ideal for that target platform. My go-to is Sprout's always up-to-date social sizes: https://sproutsocial.com/insights/social-media-image-sizes-guide/.

If you're not a designer or photographer yourself, look to the web for help. You can use Canva (www.canva.com) for graphic design, and it also will help you optimize your images for different social media. I like Adobe Spark and sometimes use Photoshop when I want a bit more control over an image. I use a number of free stock photo sites (www.pexels.com is a favorite of mine) to get great images.

When Should I Post?

One wonderful thing about social media is that you can schedule posts out over the next few months, with everything lined up and ready to go.

For scheduling software, you've got a lot of options. You can use the native scheduling on Facebook, of course. I've worked a fair bit with Sprout Social, and it's one of several really solid applications. Hootesuite and Missinglettr are others we rely on. You can select profiles that you want to post to — your LinkedIn, Facebook, Instagram, Twitter, everything — and schedule future posts to those profiles. Once you connect your profiles to the system, the process is incredibly easy.

You've got posts scheduled out for the next weeks and months. Then if something happens organically, you can go ahead and post. But if it doesn't, or you get busy, you know that posts are set up and you're covered.

Summary

If you're digging in for the first time, keep these tips in mind and go for it! Be your authentic self and get out there.

If you've tested the waters of social media without a lot of success, use a few of the above tactics to change up or refresh your approach. You might just transform your social presence.

Whether you love social media or not, I think we can all agree that it's part of business today. You can use it to get new leads, run retargeting ads to prospects to add more marketing touches, and to wow clients with special groups and increased engagement. Social is also a great way to get someone through the Know, Like, Trust cycle. It's fine to start small – just start!

Chapter 5: Quick Review

- Social media puts you where your customers and prospects are.

- Wherever your customers are, you should be there, too.

- Credibility and authenticity. Social media is a uniquely effective tool in helping people get to know you, like you, and trust you.

- Social proof. People buy from people they like.

- If you're wondering what to post, make a list of questions that you often get from prospective and existing customers.

- How to write it? Make it sound like a conversation, something you'd actually say to someone.

- Social media image sizes: Learn more about this at https://sproutsocial.com/insights/social-media-image-sizes-guide/.

- Schedule a slew of posts within the social platform or using a tool.

- Whether you love social media or not, it's part of business today. Just starting? It's fine to start small. Just start!

➡☐ Join the 7 Marketing Basics Facebook group here: https://www.facebook.com/groups/7marketingbasics/.

CHAPTER 6

MAKING IT HAPPEN WITH AUTOMATION

Small, repetitive, continuous actions, chained together, build momentous momentum.

— Mike Michalowicz

Once you see the opportunities (holes) in your business and start by applying one or two marketing basics, then using some automated systems just makes sense. It's so 80/20.

While "marketing automation" refers to the software platforms and technologies that automate repetitive tasks and make it easier to market across multiple channels, there is definitely a human side to it.

Working with this technology, you can be more effective in connecting with other people and in exposing the humanity of your business. And, ultimately, that's what sales and marketing is all about!

Really, you just need to be able to connect with and relate to other people. Marketing automation helps you to start and maintain a conversation. (This is especially important when working with a long buying cycle!) It allows you to put your voice into your marketing.

Connecting With Automation

How can you build marketing automation into your everyday activities to become more efficient and effective?

You can use a voice recorder or dictation app to capture notes and impressions. To capture information on a business card, use your smartphone's camera and text recognition processing to automate entry of contact details. Take a photo too so that you can be sure to recognize a new contact the next time you meet.

Create a follow-up email that will go out at the end of day to the folks who stopped by your booth earlier. You might add a photo of your booth team, or present links to various products or solutions so that they can opt in for further information — and basically self-segment and move themselves along the sales funnel. Just check in briefly, offer helpful or engaging content, and mention that you'll follow up to find out if they have any questions.

Automation also makes it easy for you to combine multiple media and platforms — email, text, trade shows, phone calls, in person, demos, webinars — to create a multitouch campaign. If done well, it allows you to change the way people see the world so that your company is part of their world view.

Advanced Learning Opportunity

I created a master class on the strategies you've been reading about here. Because you have this book, you can access it for free if you scan the QR code below or text MASTERCLASS to +1 530-203-5703.

Small businesses can really excel with marketing automation because they're agile and pros at person-to-person interaction. But many such companies are afraid to use technology in their marketing systems because they don't want to seem impersonal or they think it's unaffordable. They've always sold a certain way, and they are worried that a system will change how they do things, or that it won't work, or that it will cost too much.

What I came to realize after years of working with small businesses is that sustained conversations (enabled by automation!) between these businesses and their customers allow them to get to know, like, and trust one another. This is so important that I now help many of my clients run "Know, Like, Trust" marketing automation campaigns. It's a great way to keep the conversation going, build relationships, and make sure that no prospect falls through the cracks.

The tracking and targeting tools you can find within marketing automation systems give you tremendous benefits as well. (Talk about doing more with less!) You can track behavior before you have a relationship with a contact and then use that intelligence to focus your marketing on them in a smart and useful way.

What's Changed? Why Now?

Why is now the time to look at marketing automation? I've seen two big reasons it's a good fit for my clients, and they just might apply to you and your business as well.

First, an investment in marketing automation pays off. This is true not only because automation has become so much more common and affordable, but also because it delivers results. In my experience I've seen that for every dollar you put into automation, you'll get $5, $10, or $100 out. It's so exciting to see this technology helping small companies to be more successful!

When I first started digging into this topic, my friend Frank offhandedly said, "Infusionsoft is the cheapest and best employee I've ever had!" He was talking about how he uses marketing automation to stay in touch with clients, follow up with his prospects, automatically collect monthly fees, and promo his events – 24/7. So great. It's like you can't afford NOT to do it!

Second, the way people buy has changed, with purchase decisions now relying heavily on online research before and personal interaction takes place. You know this story because you probably buy this way, too. So, maybe you've responded to this trend by putting some PDFs and videos on your website, but these days you need to do more.

People still need 7 or 11 or 27 touches before they buy, but those touches are not just phone calls and trade shows meetings like they used to be. Now these touches include email and website and social media, and they need to be targeted and orchestrated according to the different interests and actions of your prospects.

And did I mention lead scoring?! It's so very fabulous to keep score of people clicking on email links and engaging with your content – that way you know who's really interested! Lead scoring helps me know who to call on any given day. I'm a total fan of lead scoring.

You've seen larger companies, such as Amazon and Apple, use automation, and you can put the same tools to work for your business — to generate new leads, follow up better, and get sales faster. You can make sure you've not leaving money on the table.

Getting Started

While I've seen automation work wonders for my clients, I endorse it with two caveats.

First, I think it's best to implement automation only if or when you feel you understand every element involved. I don't mean that you need to know all the ins and outs of the automation system itself. Rather, I'm saying that it's helpful if you can manually perform the tasks — sending an email, offering a download link, etc. — that you'll be asking automation to do for you.

My second word of warning for you is to use automation only if you need it! If you've got a very simple manual process that works and doesn't require a lot of time or energy on your part, consider sticking with it. (If it's not broken, don't fix it.)

With those warnings out of the way, let's look at what marketing automation can do to simplify your life.

When I start a new client on automation, we generally set up some quick wins. Using the Know, Like, Trust model, we'll immediately offer a checklist, guide, white paper, or video. We'll set up a mix of evergreen emails along with trade shows, events, and webinars, all tied together and timed by automation. Then maybe throw in a campaign that automatically asks clients or customers for a Google review or referrals.

I find it helpful to think about any action a prospect might take and then set up some kind of automation to respond to that action in order to keep the momentum going.

Say, for example, a prospect signs up to attend your webinar. Wouldn't it be great if this person automatically got a welcome message and a calendar invite. How about a text/SMS reminder 20 minutes before the event starts.

If you offer a white paper or guide, wouldn't it be nice to let someone else worry about handling positive requests for a download? Or for following up with prospects to check in and encourage further action?

When you're presenting at a trade show or event, how cool would it be if registered participants got the option of texting a keyword to you — right there and then — for further information. (We all know they'll forget to do it later.)

The fact is that you're not going to do all this manually. You can't, and you probably don't want to. It's simply not feasible. And it's not a good use of your time!

Automation takes care of all these steps, ensuring that no prospect falls by the wayside. Equally important, automation can help you gather valuable information about who is engaging with you and your marketing outreach.

Wouldn't it be nice to know who came to the webinar and who didn't? Who actually downloaded your white paper, and who might need a reminder to check it out? Automation can manage these processes and take action based on each prospect's engagement with your marketing outreach.

Marketing automation can help all this happen smoothly, with a minimum of effort. That's why I'm a fan. When you're looking at 80/20, automation plays a vital role in making that 20% really make an impact.

Your Marketing Workflow With Automation

Sometimes automation is a bit easier to understand when you look at the big picture. Stepping back, you can see a series of basic elements driving your marketing workflow.

- Your existing contacts are loaded into a database, or CRM, where they are tagged with their interests, such as new HD technology or cool design services.

- New prospects are added to the database automatically and tagged by their specific interests (based on how they interacted with your marketing efforts).

- Emails, videos, and white papers specific to your prospect's needs are sent out in predetermined intervals.

- You get information about which emails and content your prospect has opened, which helps you to know what they are interested in. Leads can even be scored based on this information. (Learn more about lead scoring in the Q&A at the end of the book!)

- Automatic segmentation of your prospects into groups based on their specific interests allows you to deliver better information.

- Prospects will turn to you as the industry expert and will happily talk with your salespeople when they are ready to take the next steps toward purchasing.

Optimizing Your Use of Automation

By its nature, automation provides a system that can be tested and refined to deliver results. With automation in place, you can establish formal campaigns based on your data and experiences from earlier campaigns.

You can move away from a reliance on institutional knowledge or company folklore and toward repeatable, optimized campaigns. You can work smarter and be more efficient.

How will your life change? You will:

- Be notified automatically when a prospect wants a quote, demo, or sales call.

- Get the data you need to understand which emails most successfully engaged your prospects.

- Know what stage of the sales pipeline every prospect is in, and what actions occur next.

- Have all your contacts from all sources consolidated and organized in a central CRM database.

- See all your prospects segmented based on their interests.

- Watch as automation nurtures your prospects into sales-readiness by providing the information they want and need. (And they will love you for it!)

What Can You Automate?

You can and should stop doing repetitive tasks. When repetitive processes are automated, you can instead devote time to what you love and what you do best! There are dozens of tasks that are repetitive, don't get done, or could be done more efficiently.

What things do you find yourself doing over and over again? If you had a system, could you delegate that task to a colleague or automate it?

If you doubt you can find something within your own marketing efforts to automate, think again. Surely something in this list applies ....

Automate This!

LEADS

Contact requests	Inbound call sales rep assignment
Call back every customer	SMS messaging
Capture leads with free newsletter	

SALES

Sales pipeline starter kit	Focus on your hottest leads
Long term prospect nurture	New customer welcome and wow

E-COMMERCE

Generate repeat sales	Turn abandoned carts into sales
Collect all recurring billings	

CUSTOMER SERVICE & ENGAGEMENT

Contact me bubble up	Appointment reminder
Satisfaction survey	Refer a friend
Clean your contact list	Easy password recovery
Birthday reminders	Grow your social following

EVENTS

Event registration & follow-up	Facebook event promotion

OFFICE MANAGEMENT

Automate a task-driven process	W-9 collection
Easy hiring	

☐

Chapter 6: Quick Review

- Consider using some automated systems in your marketing — it's a very 80/20 thing to do! Use automation to do repetitive tasks and to be sure leads and tasks don't get forgotten. Use your human skills to do what you love and what you do best. Or just have more free time.

- While "marketing automation" refers to the software platforms and technologies that automate repetitive tasks and make it easier to market across multiple channels, there is definitely a human side to it.

- Marketing automation can be your cheapest and best employee.

- Lead scoring is a valuable method of tracking engagement. It's great for prioritizing who to focus on!

- You can automate lead follow-up, lead collection, SMS messaging, event registrations, and so much more.

➡☐ I created a master class on the strategies you've been reading about here. Access it for free by texting MASTERCLASS   to +1 530-203-5703.

CHAPTER 7

THE MARKETING BASICS CHALLENGE

If you wait until everything lines up, it's over.

— Reshma Saujani

So, which part of your business would get the biggest 80/20 boost from one of the 7 Marketing Basics? Where do you want to start?

Target + Attract   Collect Leads   Educate + Help   Offer + Close   Wow + More!   Get Referrals

When you look at your Lifecycle Marketing Master Plan — at how people find out about you, decide to buy, become your customer, and beyond — where are the holes, the opportunities?

Are you ready to take the next step?

Read on! Here's a challenge to take you forward.

Challenge Part One:

Take 10 minutes or so and write down what you've got in place now in your business for each part of the Lifecycle Marketing Master Plan. If you don't have anything in place for one of the sections, then make a big "O" for opportunity in that spot.

For example, you might have tactics in place that target + attract, and you might have a system in place for collecting leads, but not have a way to educate your prospects. Write it down! (You can write here in the book if you want!)

Challenge Part Two:

You will have one or more O's in your Lifecycle Marketing Master Plan. Choose one, any one. If you feel one is easier and will get you a quick win, choose that one first.

Choose one of the 7 Marketing Basics to fill that hole. Don't worry, you can keep it simple to start with. Just pick one and start.

For example, if you need a way to educate + help, you could choose a webinar or sales from a white paper/checklist/guide.

Set a date on which you will offer your webinar or white paper/checklist/guide. This date should be two to three weeks out at the most!

Challenge Part Three:

Follow the plan in the book. Feel free to keep it simple and pare it down. Get a quick win, and get it out there! You got this!

CHAPTER 8

YOU GOT THIS!

Remember, business is math, and math is easy;
therefore, business is easy!

— Lindsey Ardmore

I'm so happy you've reached this last chapter in the 7 Marketing Basics. Whether you've skimmed the whole book or focused on a few of the tools and tactics most interesting to you, you've probably picked up some knowledge that can help you do less and sell more.

I have used these same tools to earn mid-six figures by working half as much. Using these tools for my own business, I was able to double my sales and double my leads. And that is something that you can do too.

If you're starting at zero and you want to get going — awesome!

If you're experienced and want to level up your digital marketing skills – wonderful!

You've now got the knowledge you need to make it work.

Maybe you're responsible for marketing at your company, or maybe you're the person in charge of the business, or maybe it's your own business. Whatever the case, these 7 Marketing Basics will work for you and the business. They get results.

Take a real shot at putting even one of these 7 Marketing Basics into action, and I think you'll be amazed.

What differentiates these 7 Marketing Basics from other plans or strategies is that they are built on clear steps with a logical progression. You don't need a lot of experience to put them into practice. You just need to do it! And buying this book was your first step.

Sure, I know I'm not alone when I look at bookshelves with titles for "Dummies" and everything "Made Easy." Good intentions only go so far if they aren't backed by action. But the beauty of the 7 Marketing Basics is that they offer a framework for doing many of the things you already do — but doing them better.

You already use email to connect with your customers. You already have a website with information about your business and products or services.

You're probably already on social media — perhaps it's Facebook with friends and family; Twitter to keep up with news, memes, and your favorite personalities; Instagram to share images of the things you like and love; or LinkedIn for you or your business.

Any and all of these experiences will be valuable as you put the 7 Marketing Basics to work for your business. Now you just need to focus that experience and dedicate that work to the 20% of marketing that will deliver your 80% results.

Commit to using just one of these Marketing Basics, and you'll find yourself closer to the life you want to have. More success, more money, more time with family, more time for your hobbies.

If you're ready to automate all those manual tasks involved in marketing, start now! Move away from the grunt work. Give yourself more time to focus on other aspects of business, your career, your life.

Why This? Why Now?

What do you stand to gain by trying the 7 Marketing Basics? I don't even know where to start! It's more a question of the opportunities you'll lose if you don't give it a try. It's about how you can stop struggling from day to day and start to bring consistency to your work — and even your sales and revenues.

I've been there, and you probably have been too. For me, it was working 15-hour days, white-knuckling my way through in my corporate marketing role while trying to be Super Mom to my awesome daughter and a great partner to my sweet husband. I thought I was the picture of success, having and doing it all. But in truth, I was scrambling.

While I was grateful to have clients and be making money, I was overwhelmed and stressed. Even on vacation, I'd be busy working away. My family would find me in the hotel bathroom in the middle of the night trying to finish up a client project. Client emails and calls took priority. My boundaries with clients were horrible, and sometimes I let them run me ragged. It took a toll on my health and stressed my relationships.

Looking back, I see that I was embarrassed that it was all so hard. I was reinventing the wheel over and over again, but I couldn't see any other way. I had responsibilities and people counting on me. It was tough to make a break from all that. But once I did … wow, did things change for me.

I stepped out on my own and started using the marketing tools you've learned about in this book. I helped my clients put them to work. I pulled in six figures within the first six months!

Still, those were early days. I had just begun to formulate my 7 Marketing Basics, and the tools I offered were a huge success for my clients. But I was so busy helping clients put them to use that I hadn't applied them to my own business.

I was making great money, but I was still doing too much work. I hadn't made any more time for me and for my family. You know, things like sleeping, eating properly, and just enjoying the people I love.

Once I finally realized what was going on, I decided it was time to embrace all these tools and really make them my own. This is how the Lifecycle Marketing Master Plan was born. It changed my life, and I'm confident it will change yours.

I was a marketing automation expert before going all-in on the Lifecycle Marketing Master Plan and adopting it for my business. You'd think I would have been running my business in an automated way, but the fact is that it doesn't happen all on its own.

You need to make a conscious choice to take on your marketing work in a smarter, more thoughtful, and more efficient way. Without that focus, and without specific tools, your efforts will be scattershot. (Mine sure were!) They just won't add up to the results you can get through consistent use of proven tools, such as the 7 Marketing Basics.

I figured out, step by step, what worked for me — the tools and techniques that were both easy and effective. I created systems and processes that supported my business, my life, and my family. Turns out, these tools and systems work for pretty much everyone. By now, I've seen hundreds of clients simplify their marketing while boosting their results. And for some clients, this new approach has been life-changing.

What's my point? I learned all this stuff the hard way, but you don't have to. And the sooner you start with the 7 Marketing

Basics, the sooner you can stop struggling to make money. You can leave behind the feast-or-famine cycle with sales. You can lower your hours and bring up your productivity, hit or exceed your quotas, and increase your income.

Why Will the 7 Marketing Basics Work for You?

What's the secret to making the 7 Marketing Basics work? The tools themselves are proven winners. But there is more to it than that.

You know already that the 7 Marketing Basics will save you time. What might not be so obvious is that these tools bring success even without massive amounts of traffic or a massive ad spend. They work even on a relatively small scale. You don't need to have a ton of clients, but you do need to reach out to prospects and customers in a way that will foster success, and that's where the 7 Marketing Basics and the Lifecycle Marketing Master Plan come into play.

There is another reason you can apply the 7 Marketing Basics to your work and expect success: You don't need complex technology or the backing of a giant team. You can do it all yourself without feeling as though you're doing it all.

And there is one more reason that's less tangible, but I love it. I have found that I actually make more money when I'm happier. By putting the Lifecycle Marketing Master Plan and 7 Marketing Basics to use in my own business, I gave myself the time I wanted and needed to focus on other parts of life. I don't miss all the stress or the sleepless nights, and I find that I have more energy and enthusiasm when I do put time into my business and my clients. I think you'll find the same to be true for you.

What Will Success Look Like for You?

I know what success with the 7 Marketing Basics and Lifecycle Marketing Master Plan looked like for me and for the many clients I've advised over the years. So, I can give you a pretty good picture of what might happen for you and your business.

When you start to implement these tools, you'll be building campaigns that help people to know, like, and trust you. You might be welcoming someone new into your community or solidifying your relationship with existing customers.

Through a series of "invite sequences," you'll give people the opportunity to take the next step. You'll let them raise their hands and say, "Yes, I want your solution guide," or "Yes, I will join you for a webinar." With these steps, people will become that much more engaged, moving further down the yellow brick road of becoming your customer.

To keep your company and solutions present in the lives of these prospects and customers, you'll use an evergreen nurture campaign to connect. An email every once in a while to offer useful information, tell them about any new products or services they might like, or let them know you're still interested in providing solutions to their needs.

Once you implement the 7 Marketing Basics and set them in motion, you'll find they start to roll along with their own momentum. Especially when powered by marketing automation, these tools can build relationships even while you're off doing what you love to do most — spending time at the beach, hiking in the mountains, or enjoying a meal or gathering with your favorite people.

How to Get Started

You just need to believe and act! One thing that's so powerful about the tools we're discussing is that it just won't cost you a lot of time and money to give them a try. While it may take a little time to build real momentum, you're likely to get some wins right out of the gate.

In fact, this is one of my favorite parts of working with new clients — seeing the reaction when their first foray into the 7 Marketing Basics brings results that exceed all their hopes and expectations!

Many of these clients choose to embrace the Lifecycle Marketing Master Plan not just as a roadmap but also as a priority list that guides them step by step in connecting with customers. Like them, you can use it every day to reaffirm that the basic needs of your business and your prospects and clients are being met. Put it in place, and your business will immediately begin to change.

Leads will start to come through the door. You'll notice that people are indeed starting to know, like, and trust you. Customers will inquire about quotes without such an uphill process on your end. They will love you for taking the time to listen to their needs and for regularly offering up valuable insights and information to help their business thrive.

I know that if you look back through this book, pick a Marketing Basic that feels comfortable, and take steps to put it into action, you will find success. You'll grow your company and career.

Dive into the Lifecycle Marketing Master Plan and make it your own. Commit to a first step. Update your business profile on social media. Look through your company's files to find content you can transform into an asset such as a guide, checklist, or white paper. Jot down a few notes about a possible webinar topic, or a few people who might make good partners for an engaging presentation.

After you take this first step, move on to the next! Every one of these Marketing Basics relies on skills that you already have — and others you can readily develop. Putting them together in the right way is critical, but the formula is right here in this book.

As they old saying goes, "There's no time like the present." Jump in and get going!

Your Master Plan for Success (A Quick-Start Guide)

Step 1: Identify your ideal customer avatar, ICA, and what they want.

This isn't something you just think about. Create a document in which you include the person's name, demographic, hobbies, and priorities. What does this person care about? What are their values? What do they like to do?

After you define exactly who they are, make a note of what you're doing to attract them. Are you generating that great content they want?

Step 2: Assess your existing lines of communication.

Are you on social media? At this point in time, every business has to do some social media basics. How would you score yourself on word of mouth? Where are you on shows, whether in-person or virtual? Where are you on articles? Do you already create and share lead magnets, such as guides, checklists, white papers, or other sources of technical information?

Step 3: Collect, store, and score your leads.

This sounds like a no brainer, but I talk with people every day who literally have a stack of business cards, or random sticky notes, or contacts haphazardly stored on their phone. That's not going to cut it!

Don't waste opportunities by letting leads slip through the cracks. Pull them off your phone and into a database. Dedicate a little time to data entry and recycle those business cards and sticky notes.

You'll want to find a way to score your leads so that you know which are hot, which are warm, and which are not. Marketing automation systems can do this for you as you generate new leads, but a manual system will work as you begin to organize existing leads.

Step 4: Create your lead follow-up best practices.

You want to offer value to your prospects right from the start. So, think about the top five questions you get about your service or industry and use them to create a download or short video that delivers information they are likely to want or need.

Step 5: Create an experience by which your perfect customer can learn from you.

Do you have this piece in place right now? Are you addressing the top questions or objections people have before they become your customer? Before they make a purchase?

If not, now's the time. Answer those questions in a fact sheet or a web page — someplace people can get the information they need to learn in order to become your customer. Think about what worldview they need to have. What technology do they have to understand? Right?

Step 6: Set yourself up to offer and sell.

You might think, "I know how to sell. I'm good." If so, that's great. While this is a huge piece of the puzzle, it's an element of sales and marketing that many people overlook. They simply don't provide an easy way for someone to try out the product or service they offer. So, if you haven't already, take a look at your services and see what options work for your business.

Once a prospect is ready to buy, is it easy for them to follow through? Can they just send you a payment and be done, or do you have a complex invoicing and payment process? Try to eliminate any friction here so that the process is fast, intuitive, and painless for your new customer. You also want a mechanism in place that will help you follow up with anyone who doesn't complete a purchase.

Step 7: Follow up after the sale.

A quick phone call to see how the customer likes the product and service is good in so many ways. For one, you can make sure the solution is actually meeting their needs. In doing so, you're also letting the customer know that you still care about their needs and plan to be there to support them. They will love you that much more!

Approach this step by thinking about how you can over-deliver and continue to help your customer. Make getting in touch a week or two after the purchase a fixed part of the overall sales process. Don't forget that your current clients are also your best prospects for future sales!

Step 8: Solicit feedback, referrals, or recommendations.

As you check in with your customers to see how they like the product or service you've provided, you can use a survey to gather information that may be useful for future marketing communications. In some cases you can go ahead and ask the customer if they would be interested in recommending you to a friend.

Not everyone appreciates surveys and requests for ratings or recommendations, so proceed carefully. One way to get customers to opt into this type of relationship is to set up a program where your best customers get rewards. It's a win for everyone involved!

Use these basic steps to apply the Lifecycle Marketing Master Plan to your own business. If you follow each of them, you will create a great system that helps you design your life and your business the way you want them to be.

Now, it's time to stop dreaming about having your successful company business work and start taking more action to get you there. You got this!

BONUS MATERIALS AND RESOURCES

Understanding the
Customer Journey

Stepping Through the Sales Funnel

The sales funnel is the journey your prospects and customers take toward a sale. If you optimize your "touches" all along this journey, you increase the likelihood that your marketing efforts will result in sales.

At the very top of your sales funnel, the broad end, are people who just are finding out about you. At the tip of the funnel, the narrow end, is the happy customer who has made a purchase. Your job is to help guide prospects from one end of the funnel to the other.

Working backward from the happy customer outcome, ask yourself what had to happen for this sale to take place. What do your customers typically do right before they buy? Do they download a demo, download a user guide, or talk to a salesperson?

Moving out toward the wide end of the funnel, ask yourself what prospects need to know about your company, product, or services before they can become customers. Do they need a deeper understanding of how a particular technology works? Or how to implement a new workflow or system?

Depending on the business you're in, this information needn't be product- or service-specific. It should help educate prospects and give them information they need and can use. By providing this information, you offer value while setting yourself up as an expert.

Once you find the most common answers to these questions, you can refine your sales funnel to address your ideal customer. Using various Marketing Basics, you can drive prospects toward those activities that most often precede a sale. Along the way you can leverage email, text messaging, phone calls (old school but proven!), automation, and all your favorite tools to keep the conversation moving forward.

Recall the basics of the Lifecycle Marketing Master Plan: attract, sell, wow. Now apply those ideas to different parts of the customer journey, and think about how your 7 Marketing Basics can help!

As they move into the sales funnel, prospects will wind up qualifying — or disqualifying — themselves on their own. Whether or not they ultimately decide they want and need your product or service, you will have provided them with value and cemented your reputation as a helpful expert.

On one end, the bottom, or tip, of the funnel, you have a happy customer who has made a purchase and who loves you. The top, or broad end, of the funnel is where you attract and engage customers. That's where your work begins.

Marketing and Sales Strategy
From David Meerman Scott

Web Strategy Diagram

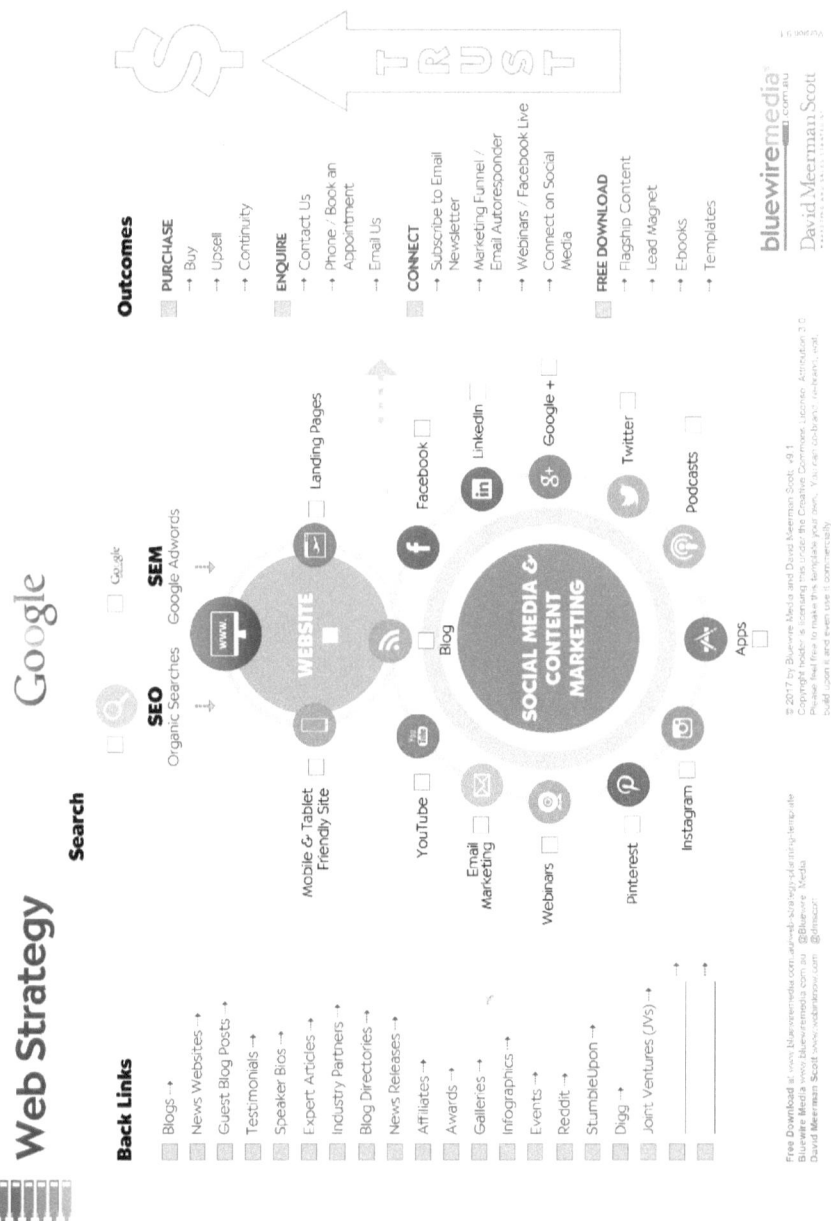

Finding 'Holes' and Opportunities in Your Marketing

Lifecycle Marketing Master Plan

You can download your Master Plan here:
https://7marketingbasicsstart.com

Lifecycle Marketing
Master Plan

Target + Attract	Collect Leads	Educate + Help	Offer + Close	Wow + More!	Get Referrals
Identify your ideal customer + give them what they want.	Set up a Sign up / Opt In system to capture all of their info.	Provide the helpful info your prospects crave. Build know, like, trust.	Make it easy for your customers to buy. Don't leave money on the table.	Welcome + follow-up system. Offer more and increase LTV	Get testimonials and referrals on demand.

Prepare for a Great Event!

Webinar Rehearsal Checklist

Beginning

About 10 minutes before you start, get attendees to engage with you in the chat box. Ask a few questions to get things going. Where are you? Can you hear me? Ask them to use the chat box to let you know. You need to teach attendees to interact with you!

Practice your open. Really! This is when attendees will decide if they like you, and if they want to stay with you for the next 30-60 minutes. Tell them what they will get, what they will learn. List out your points: A, B, and C. (Wait to talk about yourself until a bit later in the webinar.)

Pause and say, "Let's get started." Pause again for an edit point in case you will be editing the recording later.

Middle

Cover your points: A, B, and C. Recap what participants got/learned after each point. Be sure that you include any helpful links in the chat throughout the webinar.

Q&A

Put two or three questions together to have on hand in case not many come in through the chat during the main part of the webinar. Use these questions to address and/or overcome objections you often hear.

Be sure you have a colleague who can handle the Q&A. They can gather any questions that are posted to the chat, and they can also come onto the webinar and pose select questions to you during the Q&A session. Alternatively, your colleague can send you questions by text and let you manage things from there.

For any questions that you don't want to address live, it's always fine to say that you'll follow up with people offline.

Close

Review your CTA. Figure out how you plan to incorporate it into the chat and your closing slide.

Tech Check and Logistics

Confirm the back-channel communication tool you and your colleagues will be using during the webinar. (Skype, text, WhatsApp?)

Test your mic, lights, and internet. (Use a hardwired ethernet connection whenever possible to minimize bandwidth issues.)

Use a Proven Formula

Webinar Outline Template

10 Minutes Before You Start

Get people engaged with you and the chat box. Ask questions, tell stories.

"Hi! How are you?"

"Where are you today?"

"How's the weather?"

Open

Make your purpose and the subject of the webinar clear. Who is this information for, and what will they get by the end?

"Let's get started." (Pause so you have a good edit point.) "Welcome! I'm Cindy, and I'm glad you're here! Today you'll find out about A, B, and C, and by the end of our discussion, you'll know how to X, Y, and Z."

"I want to welcome my special guest/expert/friend, [insert name]. Hey, how are you today?"

"OK, let's get right into it. The other day you were talking with me about problem A. Tell me more about that."

Point 1

"Yes! I was talking with [title/type of business owner] the other day, and she said that [explain the problem and solution]."

Point 2

"I just got a call about problem B, and what [title/type of business owner] told me was that [explain the problem and solution]."

Point 3

"The other day when we were talking, you told me that your customer [title/type of business owner] was facing problem 3, and [share about the problem and solution]."

Q&A

Answer the questions that typically are the top objections. Any outlier questions can be addressed individually, offline. Have three to five questions ready to talk about, just in case you don't have a ton of engagement in the chat

Close

Talk about what participants learned today and what they can do next to apply this info and be successful with it.

CTA

Ask participants to "chat in" if they want a demo or trial, or if they are interested in jumping on a 10-minute call.

Keep It Running Smoothly

Webinar Chat Master Template

Prepare Your Chat Master

If you can, get a coworker or friend to handle the chat during the webinar. Their job is to keep people engaged, provide helpful info, and manage the Q&A.

Here's the template we use. Keep it handy as a reference during your webinar.

Webinar Info

Client/Company Name:

Webinar Name:

Webinar Date(s):

Webinar Talent/Host(s):

Back channel method for talking w host during the webinar (Skype, WhatsApp, text, other):

Webinar Details

Registration link:

Webinar join link:

Other related info:

Contact person at the client/company to call or contact during the webinar if a problem comes up:

Any other details:

Info to Post During the Webinar

Helpful links and when to post those links.

- client website URL:
- calendar links:
- data sheet:
- other:

Other bonus content, PDF, or similar to post in chat during the webinar:

Contact info of host or other key people:

CTA to post in chat during the webinar:

Additional information:

Save the chat from the webinar here:

Online or in Person,
Make It Look Professional

Video Interview and Appearance Checklist

Why Video Interviews/Appearances Are So Important

Because it's so easy today to produce a good video and get it posted almost immediately, doing interviews online or at events is part of the game. Video lets people get to know you and trust you — crucial for business!

We all know how important it is to do these video interviews, but we get nervous, right? These pro tips will make it so much easier.

Whether your company is big or small, you need to be prepared to give a great video interview.

Here's the Video Interview and Appearance Checklist I like to use. It is short and sweet, just the proven essentials that we know work: choosing what to say, preparing, and practicing, plus some totally doable pro techniques that will make your interview shine.

Choosing What to Say

Knowing what you're going to say in advance is everything.

It can feel challenging to figure out what to say during the interview, whether you're on Zoom, Skype, or in person at an event or show.

Sometimes we feel nervous or don't know what to say when press and customers come by and ask for a video interview, so let's look at choosing what to say ahead of time.

- Memorize an opening and a closing blurb. Knowing how you'll open and close is key and will really change your comfort level.

- Choose two or three points in the middle. You may not end up using them all, but have few prepared.

- Consider what you want someone to do after they view the video. What's the call to action (CTA)?

- Avoid the sales pitch. Focus on providing helpful or educational information. Maybe you have a use case and can tell the story of how using your product has solved someone's problem.

- Determine if there will be an interviewer on video with you or if it will be you solo.

Preparing and Practicing

Practicing works!

Here are some key things to think about and consider in preparation.

- Grab viewers' attention in the first 10 seconds. Say something that the viewer cares about in the very first part of the video.

- Keep it short. It's a time issue - when somebody views a piece of video content on the web or social media, they have minimal amount of time.

- Make sure that you prep and do your homework beforehand. You can do an awful lot of damage if you can't talk about your product in a good way.

- Take control. With prep you can take control of the situation.

- Be concise.

- After they view your video, what one thing would you like them to take away?

- Practice! Do a few run throughs with a colleague. Video yourself with your phone and give it a look. Don't be too critical of yourself, but notice things like "um" and consider the conciseness of your message.

Pro Techniques

Use proven techniques for a top-notch interview.

- Designate one or two people as your video interview people. If you're at a live event and someone requests an interview at an inconvenient time, offer an alternative time when your chosen representative can really be ready. It's best to have the right person on camera representing your business.

- Breathe!

- Talk with the crew or interviewer in advance. Ask them if you can pick up, if you can do another take, if will there be a B roll, if they want you to look at the camera or look off camera.

- Plan where you want to do the shoot. Know what is in the background shot, and have something behind you.

- Practice by doing a video yourself and posting it on your social media or website in advance.

- If you can't do anything with your hands, keep them clasped in front of you.

- Hold a few seconds at the end for nice edit point.

Next Steps and More

Q&A With Cindy Z.

Q. Marketing tools and social media platforms seem to be changing so quickly these days. Why do you think that the 7 Marketing Basics will stand the test of time?

The 7 Marketing Basics are fundamental strategies that remain valid over time, but the specific tools you use in implementing those strategies might change. So, for example, while we primarily use Zoom for webinars, we work with clients who use other platforms. In the future, we'll all move on to other tools. It's not so much the tools you use but rather the engaging with people, getting the info out, being in front of them on video, and building the "Know, Like, Trust" relationship.

You need to understand what kinds of information people need and when they need it before you can use tools and technology to meet that need. It's really about meeting people where they are.

Q. How do the 7 Marketing Basics apply to the remote and virtual events that have become so much more prevalent in recent times?

I've hosted countless webinars and virtual events, and I truly do believe that many of the same factors are at play when you're addressing your audience through a laptop, tablet, or smartphone screen. Sure, different types of meetings and platforms will ultimately offer different experiences, but the goal is always the same: to engage.

And when it comes to engaging people through a remote presentation or meeting, I always come back to four key points that I emphasize when I talk about one of my favorite Marketing Basics: the webinar.

7 Marketing Basics: Do Less and Sell More

1. Grab people's attention in the first 10 seconds. Say something that your audience/attendees care about in the very first part of the video.

2. Decide what one thing you would like your audience/attendees to take away from your interview or meeting.

3. Determine the one thing you'd like your audience/attendees to do after your presentation or meeting. What's the next step? Did you make it easy for them to take that next step?

4. Practice! Do a couple run throughs with a colleague. Don't be too critical of yourself. Do notice things like "um" and the conciseness of your message.

If you take care of these four things, you can host a successful online event of almost any kind with minimum work and maximum results. Of course, you'll want to be sure you're selecting the right format and technology for the event you have in mind. Get familiar with the technology and how to use it smoothly. Be aware of any security issues or bugs that could compromise your live event.

The tools for hosting remote and online events are becoming better and more sophisticated by the day. Turn your focus toward using those tools to connect and engage effectively.

Q. Content repurposing is a practice you really praise in the 7 Marketing Basics. Why is it so important and so valuable?

When you work really hard to create a video or webinar or blog post, you owe it to yourself and your business to do even more with that good work and good information. The next step is to leverage it and turn it into a dozen or more great pieces of content.

Why? Because even though you might feel as though you got your message out in that original webinar or post, the people you want to reach might not have seen it. And even if they did see it, they may have taken away just one or two key points and still could benefit from the rest of your message.

You might say, "But I already talked about that!" Or think, "I already did an email on that. I don't want to be redundant." But here's the thing: although you could explain the topic or solution in your sleep, it's probably new to your prospects. Repurposing content works because people learn from repetition, and they just can't take in every fact or detail the first time around.

And don't forget timing! Sure, a prospect might have seen your message, but did they see it at the right time for them? Or were they busy, in the middle of other things? If you put your info out there again in another way at another time, you might reach that prospect at the perfect moment.

Finally, think about the vehicle or medium you're using. Some folks prefer video, while others want to read. You serve prospects and clients best when we put out your messages in ways that make it easy — and even enjoyable — for them to consume.

Q. Do you need to create a ton of content to make the Lifecycle Marketing Master Plan work?

Not really! What you're actually doing is using a few pieces of content in many different ways.

If repurposing content to create a bunch of different "assets" feels daunting to you, approach it from the flip side. Just do one thing. Do just one webinar or create just one checklist.

Once you've done that piece, you'll find you can quite quickly and easily leverage it in a new way. You can turn a checklist into a blog or an email. You can slice and dice a recorded webinar to create video or audio clips, and then use those to engage with prospects and customers.

All the while, you're doing less work and increasing the impact of your marketing efforts. You're making the most of that 80/20 Rule!

Q. **It takes me forever to write anything, and I don't really like doing it. Where do I start in writing an email targeted to my prospects and leads, and what do I say? Help!**

There are three W's involved in writing a really great email. The first is "what." What is the purpose of this email? Identify a single purpose. Don't try to pack in a ton of information. Just ask yourself what you want your customers to do after they read the email. Use this as your focus and as your call to action at the end of your email.

Also think about what you want your prospects to believe about your product or service, or how you can help them, and if you can embed that message into the email?

Along those same lines, consider the "What's in it for me?" (WIIFM) aspect, or what value you're providing to readers. Answer the unspoken question: Why should I read this? Think about a specific customer — someone you work with in real life — and what would interest that person right out of the gate. That first sentence has to be super-interesting to your reader.

Go ahead and start with "Hello" and then the person's first name. You can also personalize your message by mentioning the last time you talked or a solution you know they're already interested in.

In terms of writing style, keep it conversational. Despite what you might have learned in school, using "I" and "you" — especially "you" — is the way to go. In fact, go ahead and count the number of "you" and "your" versus "I," "we," and "us." Lean heavily on "you"!

As you wrap up, be sure to include your name along with your usual signature including all your contact information.

Q. SEO still seems to be a critical part of marketing effectively. Why isn't SEO part of the 7 Marketing Basics? (And do you have any SEO advice to offer?)

The 7 Marketing Basics may not be the end all, be all for you, but they work! Having said that, other tools and tactics — including SEO — can be effective too.

Every small business wants sales, and sales come from talking and engaging with people. To me, that comes before SEO. If you're paying attention to what you're putting on your website and making sure it provides the information your prospects need to have, then the right content (SEO-wise) will be there on the website. Once you put your sales conversation into your marketing, it should find its way into all your content.

Because SEO isn't my primary focus, I refer anyone who wants more insight to Neil Patel and Eric Siu, whose Marketing School is online at https://marketingschool.io/.

Q. Maintaining a good website is obviously a must. If you were to provide just a few tips for businesses looking to do better with their websites, what would you say?

When you look at your website, you want to be sure it tells prospects four things: who you are for (so they think, "Oh, that's me!"), what problem you solve ("That's my problem!"), what you want them to believe, and what you want them to do next. And it all has to be there, "above the fold," on the front page.

You also want to include a call to action. Oftentimes, I'll suggest a big ask and a small ask. "Book an appointment" might be the big ask, and a download opportunity might be the small ask.

Q. I'm not sure I really understand lead scoring. Could you explain it in a bit more detail?

Lead scoring is an amazing way to track engagement. Wouldn't it be nice to know who opens your emails, what they click on, and if they have visited your website? Lead scoring helps with this, and more.

While keeping track of engagement is great, lead scoring also allows you to put a rubric in place that assigns points to different actions, So, if a prospect opens an email, that might be one point. Clicking on a link might be three points, and signing up for a webinar might be five points. Use whatever works best for you! By ranking your prospects according to the criteria you value most, this lead scoring system helps to you prioritize your day and know whom to call first.

Q. I know these are marketing *basics*, but some of them seem a bit hard to me. Do you have any advice?

Yes, it can seem like a lot. I remind my clients more than once that they don't need to do all these at once, and that seems to help.

You can do just the bare minimum, and it will make a difference!

For example, just make sure you have a Facebook page for your company and that you post once a week. Or, write an email to send out to your business contact list once a month. If you're not comfortable with a webinar, just do a meeting with a few people. Choose a discussion topic, send out an invite to three or four people the day before, and just have a conversation.

If you feel as though you'd like even more guidance, check out the 7 Marketing Basics website (www.7marketingbasics.com) and training course.

Q. You give so many options for getting started with the 7 Marketing Basics. In your opinion, what is the absolute simplest, easiest, and fastest first step a person could take?

I answer this question differently depending on who's asking! For many clients, I suggest they start with what they've got.

"I need more leads" is something I hear all the time. And yes, new leads are great. That said, too many people are trying to get new leads, but not really doing anything with the leads they have. Sometimes the quickest sales and marketing win is in the leads and customers you have now.

So, your first step is to determine if you need help getting new leads or help following up with existing leads. Once you know this, focus on coming up with something of value that you can give to these people.

An easy way to do that is to think about the top five questions you get about your service or industry and use them to put together a checklist, a one-page report, or even a video where you talk with a co-worker or customer. Do what's most comfortable for you! Pick whatever is easiest for a quick win. (And, after you create one piece of content, you can turn it into another!)

Deliver that content to your prospects or leads, follow up to see how they liked it and if it was useful, and then keep that conversation going — hopefully toward a sale!

Need a bit of a boost? Check out the Marketing Basics Challenge chapter!

ACKNOWLEDGMENTS

Very special thanks to my family: Maya, Gary, Jean, and Kathleen, and to my parents, Kay and Bob.

I am so grateful to Kitty Higinbotham, who brought the clarity needed to take my ideas and turn them into this book. Her writing skills, vision, and encouragement are priceless.

Special thanks to my partners, team, and colleagues at Kokoro Marketing and Dundee Hills Group: Amy Gaylord, Bob Decker, Caryn Cohen, Chris Lesieutre, Fallon Cavanagh, Jenna Elegante, Kristin Berkery, and Pat Brown.

Finally, a shout out to the friends and colleagues who graciously invested their time and energy inspiring me and providing feedback on early drafts of the book. To Barbara Jones, Bill Crawford, Bob Kovacs, Cami Shieff, Carol White, Chris Krugler, Danna Mann, David Cohen, Frank Bloksberg, Jillian Littlejohn, Jim Jachetta, Kathy Swanson, the Keap/Infusionsoft staff who taught me about marketing automation, Kevin Joyce, Lee Goff, Leigh Kohlmann, Linda Hensel, Lindsey Ardmore, MC Patel, Rick Smith, Ryan Chapman, Saifudin Sani, Sam Bennett, Shell Vera, Stephane Billat, and Wes Schaeffer: Thank you!

ABOUT THE AUTHOR

Cindy Zuelsdorf grew up in one of the highest-pressure business environments: broadcast television. In an industry fueled by high-touch, face-to-face relationships, she cut her teeth selling tech to companies ranging from NBC to NASA. After years spent mastering old-school techniques, she discovered sales and marketing automation — and that's when she realized she had the tools and knowledge to help small businesses reap big rewards through their marketing efforts.

Today Cindy Z. — via her agency, Kokoro Marketing — helps small businesses across a wide array of verticals to optimize marketing and realize meaningful results with a minimum of work. Kokoro (www.kokoroinc.com) specializes in taking scattered technical platforms and transforming them into a finely tuned, time-saving, revenue-generating engine that builds authentic connections with people.

Want More 7 Marketing Basics?

If you want to transform your company and exceed your marketing goals, and don't know where to start — but don't want to hire a marketing agency to do it for you — then the 7 Marketing Basics Course might be for you.

Does this sound familiar?

- You need to do marketing for your company or business, have way too much to do, feel overwhelmed, or are not sure what to do next.

- You are looking to find out what's working now (not what worked years ago) in today's market.

- Driving sales with great marketing is your top priority, and you want to silence all the noise and nonsense out there.

- You're a marketing pro, and you need a great way to get and stay up to date on the newest tools and tactics while saving time and resources.

Ready to take the next step? You got this! The 7 Marketing Basics Course is the companion to this book.

You get step-by-step details for each of the seven basics so you can apply them yourself today. Self-paced, on-demand modules with videos, templates, campaigns, checklists and more.

Sign up or learn more at www.7marketingbasics.com, or text 7basics to +1 530-203-5703. Even better, join the Facebook group: https://www.facebook.com/groups/7marketingbasics/.